It's Easy T

Blues G r

by Joe Bennett

Order No. AM955196
ISBN 0-7119-8008-X

Written by Joe Bennett.
Edited by Sorcha Armstrong.
Musical examples by Richard Barrett.
Music engraving by Digital Music Art.

Book design by Phil Gambrill.
Cover design by Michael Bell Design.
Illustrations by Andy Hammond.

Specialist guitar pictures supplied courtesy of
Balafon Books (pages 88-92)
Text photographs courtesy of the following:
London Features International (Pages 4, 7,
10, 14, 16, 18, 20, 22, 25, 44, 59, 75, 87, 92)
Redferns (Pages 7, 24, 67, 85, 91, 92)
Pictorial Press (Page 28)

Printed in the United Kingdom by
Printwise (Haverhill) Limited, Haverhill, Suffolk.

John Lee Hooker: the original bluffer manages to get away with using 3 chords, a couple of string-bends and some serious frowning. **Take note!**

Introduction

Every guitarist loves the blues. It's easy to get to grips with, fun to play and (most importantly) it's a *great way to look cool*. Would Robert Johnson have sold his soul to the Devil in return for a pointy death-metal super-axe? Would Jake and Elwood have been icons for a generation if they'd been called the Jazz Fusion Brothers?

It's fairly easy to bluff your way at blues if you know a few simple tricks. For example, *don't* enjoy yourself (or if you do, don't be *seen* to enjoy yourself). This is serious, mystical music, and if you let your bluffer's facade crack for a second, people might find out that you're just playing two badly-fretted chords and some wildly inaccurate string bends.

Have an opinion, and stick to it whatever anyone says. **John Lee Hooker** only knows two scale shapes and doesn't play in time? That may be true, but he's the man, he's the dude, he was there at the start, you can hear his influence in every note **Hendrix** ever played...

Also, it's essential that you learn the language properly. Words like 'feel', 'tone', 'classic', 'authentic', 'man' and 'touch' can be combined in almost any order to make you a truly articulate blues bluffer.

Try This...

"I love that classic Clapton tone, but he's lost the touch. He used to have such an authentic feel, man".
Or how about...
"I loved Clapton's feel, but he's lost the authentic tone. He used to have such a classic touch, man."

This is 100% bluffer's gobbledegook, and best of all, anyone who disagrees "just doesn't understand the blues".

It's Easy To Bluff... Blues Guitar is a complete handbook for the bogus bluesman. Not only does it explain all the essential riffs, techniques, chords and scales you need to bluff through any gig from Louisiana to Luton, it also tells you what to wear, which albums to name-drop, and what gear to use if you're going to impress everyone in the bar afterwards (and if you were thinking of ordering a vodka and lime, put this book down now - there's no hope for you).

The Story of the Blues or 'Who to name-drop, and when'

Historians disagree amongst themselves about exactly when the blues began, but let them argue it out - anyone who's managed to get a full-time paid gig as a blues historian is a better bluffer than you or I anyway.

Early Influences

To appear knowledgeable about your blues background, you only need to drop a few names. One is that of **Robert Johnson**. Although he was by no means the first recording blues guitarist, he's almost certainly the earliest one whose licks we all steal. Bottleneck triplets? Robert was there first. Riffs changing with the chords? Bob again. From a bluffing point of view, he's a good history subject to choose because his convenient early death means you don't have too much studying to do.

The other essential names to slide subtly into conversation are those of the even earlier bluesmen (**Blind Blake**, **Blind Lemon Jefferson**, **Charley Patton**). It doesn't matter that you've never heard any music by these guys - none of the assembled company will have either, so you're on safe ground bluff-wise. If another bluffer tries to get in there with a Robert Johnson reference, just go one better with a phrase such as "yeah, Johnson was cool, but all his bottleneck licks are straight steals from Charley Patton."

The Electric players

After the early popular bluesmen - primarily Johnson and **Aaron 'T-bone' Walker** - a new wave of players arrived in the 1940s-50s. **Albert King**, **Muddy Waters**, **BB King** and **John Lee Hooker** were all electric players, so they're the earliest group of guitarists you can confidently cite as an 'influence' when you play that pentatonic lick you learned from Bon Jovi.

As the '50s and '60s progressed, the guitar sounds got dirtier and the players more flamboyant. **Albert Collins**, **Freddie King** and **Buddy Guy** held the torch for a decade or so, and although they're not as essential name-drop material as the previous generation, they did bridge the gap until...

...1965, when the British arrived. **John Mayall's Bluesbreakers**, **Cream**, and early **Fleetwood Mac** pioneered more powerful electric blues, aiding the blues/ R&B/ rock crossover that was complete by the time everyone started describing **Led Zeppelin** as a rock band.

Jimmy Page - "blues tone with a rock feel". Or should that be "rock tone with a blues feel"?

Here's another great conversation to bluff your way through. If someone describes **Jimmy Page** as a great rock guitarist, you can take the opposite stance - "man, every lick he ever played was pure blues - he just had a rock tone". You could equally defend the opposite viewpoint, of course, as long as you mix the words up a bit - "man, every lick he played was pure rock - he just had a blues feel".

Most guitarists are **Hendrix** fans to some extent, so there's little point in dropping Jimi into conversation unless you're sure of your ground. You could try some ambiguous references to his predecessors along the lines of "there's more **Muddy Waters** in his playing that most people think, you know?" but generally, steer clear of bluffsville when it comes to Hendrix.

Of the sixties greats, Clapton and Hendrix are the two about whom you need to know the most anecdotes, but it helps to have a smattering of **Peter Green** (grew really long fingernails, went a bit off the rails, comeback not as great as we hoped) and **Rory Gallagher** (wore a plaid shirt, hated effects, used Strat/AC30 combination until his death in 1995).

Rory Gallagher - "plaid shirt"

The New Generation

As the 1980s came along, many guitar players looked towards big hair and even bigger guitar sounds. A few players continued to turn out 'authentic' blues, but with an unprecedented degree of technical skill.

Robben Ford, **Stevie Ray Vaughan**, **Jeff Healey** and **Gary Moore** all produced polished, slick blues albums throughout the decade. Despite their contemporary status, it's fine for bluffing guitarists to name-drop these guys, as long as you obey the lineage rule; "man, SRV had that something - you can really hear his pain in those **Albert Collins** licks he adapted. Of course, Albert never left the house without the Lightnin' Hopkins songbook..."

Right now, we're in a bit of a blues drought. Many of the classic players are still around (**Clapton**, **Johnny Winter**, **BB King**, **Peter Green**) but there are few contemporary players bringing blues guitar playing to the mainstream record buyer. And if a great new player does come along and you've never heard of them, it's always safe to bluff your way through with this handy emergency bluffspeak phrasebook below.

Bluff Phrasebook

Use this handy table to compare any new player with any classic player. Simply mix and match the words shown here; depending on the number of guitarists you know, this can be used to create over 16 million credible blues phrases.

New Player	touch	is	genius
	pick technique	is pretty much	the best
	feel	isn't	classic
	sound	ain't	damn good
	style	sure is	hot
	album	sounds	derivative
	lineage	has gotta be	from God
	guitar playing	always was	the real thing

For example...

Clapton's - touch - sure is - the best

check out	the	Old Player	influence
feel	the classic		phrasing
listen out for	the stompin'		lick/s
you can really hear	that uncanny		spirit
you gotta feel	that unbelievable		legacy
did you get	the dude's		feel
I love	the obvious		echoes
do you buy	the amazing		style solo

you can really hear - the classic - **Muddy Waters** - legacy

The late **Jimi Hendrix**. Be careful what you say about him - you're likely to be outbluffed.

The Players

Bite-size biogs

Blues purists will consider it blasphemy to have a player's entire life summarised in one page, but in reality, you can bluff your way through with a surprisingly small amount of knowledge. In this chapter you'll find an instant guide to six top blues guitarists.

Remember that these aren't necessarily the most important or famous players - we haven't included **Gary Moore** or **Muddy Waters**, for example - but they are the names which crop up most frequently in blues gig-speak.

For each artist, I've included some basic **biographical information**, notes on **playing style**, plus (most importantly) which **techniques** you should steal in order to abet your bluffing career. Of course, you have to know the **gear** they used - remember that equipment trainspotters are everywhere and could pounce at any time.

To save you from having to wade through a truckload of albums, I've also picked out one **essential album** for you to mention (not necessarily the best-known - it can sometimes pay dividends to bluff your way by showing you listen to the obscure stuff). If you're actually asked to prove that you've heard the artist, you'd be stuck without the quick and easy '**finest moment**' reference.

Finally, because blues-speak can get pretty dogmatic, it's useful to have a few oven-ready opinions up your sleeve. For each player, I've included an 'instant opinion' (usually ambiguous enough to cover all situations) and an 'acceptable criticism'. If you're cool enough to intelligently criticise one of the greats, your status as a blackbelt blues bluffer is assured.

Robert Johnson

HISTORY AND BACKGROUND:
Born 8th May 1911, Hazlehurst Mississippi. Influenced by early blues pioneers such as **Blind Lemon Jefferson**, **Son House**, **Lonnie Johnson**. Went on to influence pretty much every electric blues and rock player, directly or indirectly, especially 1960s electric blues revolution (his songs were covered by **The Rolling Stones**, **Captain Beefheart**, and **Cream**). **Peter Green** recorded *The Robert Johnson Songbook* in 1998, an album which exclusively featured Johnson cover versions.

Recorded 32 songs in his lifetime (though there are rumours of a mythical extra 'undiscovered' track which is the blues bluffer's Holy Grail). Disappeared for some time and eventually re-emerged a much improved guitar player. Legend has it that he sold his soul to the Devil in return for his fretboard skills. Died 16th August 1938, almost certainly murdered. Conflicting stories abound that he was stabbed by a woman or a jealous husband, given poisoned whisky, or simply paid his debt to Beelzebub.

PLAYING STYLE:
Acoustic blues, fingerstyle and some bottleneck, using a variety of tunings, most related to open G (DGDGBD) with or without capo. Often plays licks in unison with the voice.

TECHNIQUES TO STEAL:

Use capos with open G tunings on guitars with high action. Try raising the first string to top G in open G (DGDGBG) with or without capo. Unison voice/guitar licks. Play triplets as downstrokes on the top two strings while moving the slide down one fret at a time for intros/outros. Use thumb for four-to-the-bar bass notes accompaniment and fingers for lead licks or chords on the top three strings.

GEAR:

Gibson L1 Acoustic Guitar, bottleneck, voice.

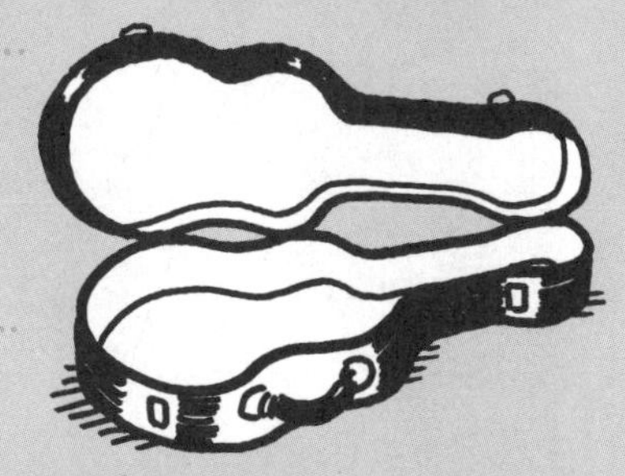

BLUFFER'S ALBUM:

Entire collected works are usually available on single CD compilations. Anything with 'rarities' or 'unreleased recordings' in the title is obviously more impressive to other bluffers.

FINEST MOMENT:

Biggest hit in his lifetime was 'Terraplane Blues' but the main accompaniment riff and lead work on 'Crossroads Blues' is arguably his most influential track.

INSTANT OPINION:

"He just had such an amazing sense of timing, y'know? The way he messes with bar-lengths to suit what was in his heart - no-one's bettered that, before or since."

ACCEPTABLE CRITICISM:

The *only* criticism allowed is that he died too young. Anything else... well, you might as well accuse the Pope of not washing his whites properly.

John Lee Hooker

HISTORY AND BACKGROUND:
According to his passport, he was born 22nd August 1917 (although he says that he was actually born in 1920, and lied about his age in order to get an army uniform to attract girls). Even though he started recording fairly late (1949), his solo career has now clocked up over 50 years. Early user of electric guitar as accompaniment. Recorded a series of classic electric blues/R&B tracks 1948-59 under various names; Johnny Lee, Johnny Williams, The Boogie Man, Texas Slim, Delta John, and Birmingham Sam and his Magic Guitar (note: add these to your list of players to name-drop). Has been 'rediscovered' at various times, most famously in 1980 when he appeared in *The Blues Brothers*, and then again in 1989 when he recorded *The Healer* with musical guests including **Carlos Santana** and **Bonnie Raitt**. Talks exclusively in unremittingly meaningless bluff-speak. Sample quotes; **"When Adam and Eve first saw each other, that's when the blues started"... "The kind of guitar I want to play is mean, mean, mean licks"... "Blues is no colour; blues is a human being. The blues, you can't see, you hear the blues"...**

PLAYING STYLE:
Responsible for the shuffle electric blues style known as 'Boogie' - basically Delta blues with a stronger pulse. Plays in the key of E a *lot*. Plenty of bass string accompaniment, with riff-based sections between vocal phrases. Throws in bars of 3/4, 5/4, 7/4 etc with gay abandon in order to make the music fit the lyrics.

TECHNIQUES TO STEAL:

Double-stop sliding licks in E. Standard E-A-G blues backing (see page 30). Keeping time by stamping your foot. Making up the lyrics as you go along. Mumbling.

GEAR:

Semi-solid f-hole guitars, often (but not exclusively) Gibson ES-335s. Reportedly 'unfussy' about amp choice.

BLUFFER'S ALBUM:

Hooker 'N Heat (1971) was a collaboration (the first of many) with Canned Heat, who have worked with 'The Hook' several times since. Best choice, though, is any compilation of his 1950s stuff.

FINEST MOMENT:

First recording 'Boogie Chillun' (1948) is most significant because it influenced so many, though 'I'm in the Mood' and 'Dimples' also feature classic Hook-isms.

INSTANT OPINION:

"There was some great stuff on *The Healer*, but why did they have to add all that big 1980s production to The Hook's sound?"

ACCEPTABLE CRITICISM:

1997 album *Don't Look Back* was repetitive and uninspired compared to previous work. But **Van Morrison** produced it, so it's OK to blame Van rather than The Hook himself.

BB King

HISTORY AND BACKGROUND:

Born Riley B King in Mississippi, Sept 16, 1925. (The 'BB' was adopted in the 1950s and stands for 'Blues Boy'). Influenced by classic bluesmen **Blind Lemon Jefferson** and **T-Bone Walker**, and jazzers **Charlie Christian** and **Django Reinhardt**. After several years spent busking in Memphis, he was asked to play on **Sonny Boy Williamson**'s KWEM radio show. In true bluff-referential style his first hit was a classic blues cover - BB's version of **Lowell Fusion**'s 'Three O'Clock Blues' topped the R&B charts at the time. Since then, he's been constantly recording as a solo artist, plus a predictable level of classic collaborations - **Buddy Guy**, **Albert Collins**, **John Lee Hooker**, **Eric Clapton** etc. He's almost certainly responsible for inventing blues/rock vibrato technique. Possibly the most influential electric blues player of all time.

PLAYING STYLE:

The man is smooth, very smooth. His entire lead style is based on bends and vib, and he rarely plays rhythm - he once told **U2**'s Edge **"I'm not too good with chords"**. Can play a complete gig with the guitar miles out of tune, using super-accurate bends to get each string exactly up to pitch.

TECHNIQUES TO STEAL:

Play a three-note lick like it was the last thing you were ever going to play. BB always 'says more with less'. Stay within absolutely safe minor pentatonic box shapes, but play them slowly, deliberately, and accurately. Don't go any lower than the 10th fret, staying beyond the 12th most of the time. Oh, and wince with a combination of joy and pain when you bend a high note.

GEAR:

Since 1958, he's played Gibson ES335s, with which he's become synonymous. He always names his guitars 'Lucille' after a girl who was the unwitting cause of a bar fight in 1949.

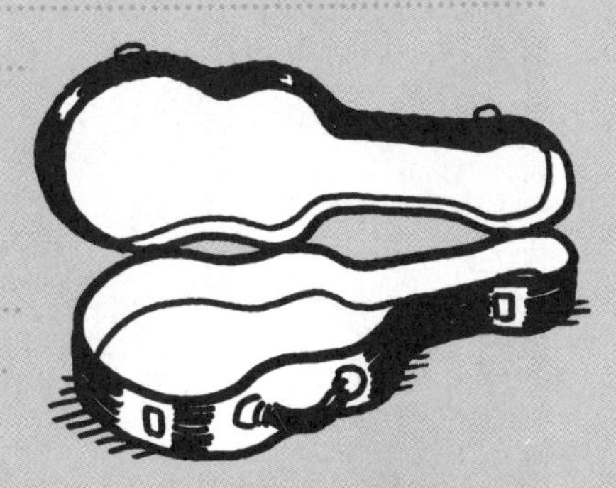

BLUFFER'S ALBUM:

He's at his best when he's playing a gig, so any live album will do. Mention *Blues Is King '67* and *Live at the Regal '65*.

FINEST MOMENT:

Arguable, but if you bring up his 1969 hit 'The Thrill is Gone' you should be fine – BB is massive amongst guitarists, but you'll rarely find one who can name more than three tracks he's recorded.

INSTANT OPINION:

"He's no Stevie Ray speed-wise, but he can sure make Lucille sing what's in his heart."

ACCEPTABLE CRITICISM:

Don't even think about it.

Jimi Hendrix

HISTORY AND BACKGROUND: Born 27th November 1942. Allegedly had his name changed by his father from Johnny Allen Hendrix to James Marshall Hendrix. Primarily perceived as a rock player, but his background, technique and note choices are typical blues. Influenced by **BB King** and **Muddy Waters**, among others. Worked with various soul/R&B acts, including **Little Richard**, **Curtis Knight**, **Ike Turner**, until he was 'discovered' by Animals' bassist **Chas Chandler**, who brought him over to the UK.

The 'Jimi Hendrix Experience' was formed in 1966 with bass player **Noel Redding** and drummer **Mitch Mitchell**. Early hits eventually led to discovery by US audiences. Notable live gigs included Monterey Pop Festival, Woodstock and the Isle of Wight Festival (the latter two occurred after Redding left in 1969). Died in his sleep, choking on his own vomit, on 18th September 1970.

PLAYING STYLE: Pyrotechnic is the word. Outrageous swooping bends, whammy bar dives, controlled (and uncontrolled) feedback, all played Very Loud Indeed. His more laid-back material features subtle grace notes using hammer-ons, and distortion dynamics controlled by plectrum picking. Made great use of the minor pentatonic scale, but solos and riffs also featured major pentatonic, Mixolydian and natural minor scales. Some techniques (e.g. thumb used to fret bass strings) relied on the fact that he had very large hands.

TECHNIQUES TO STEAL: Any of the crowd-pleasing flash techniques (e.g. playing guitar behind your head, setting guitar alight, lewd behaviour with whammy bar etc) are viewed as sacrilegious by most aficionados, so use these with care. However, any technical tricks are up for grabs - try playing trills while moving the whammy bar; moving the wah-wah while playing rapid lead licks; muted 'unpitched' chords used as a percussive effect...). Just don't admit that it's Jimi you're stealing from!

GEAR: Usually played a right-handed Strat strung left-handed and hung upside-down, through Marshall amps. Also used a variety of stompboxes, modified by English FX guru Roger Mayer. (Name drop opportunity here!)

BLUFFER'S ALBUM: Start with the 1967 Experience album *Axis: Bold As Love*, but eventually you've really got to buy them all (stay away from early-60s archive re-releases though - Jimi was rarely more than a rhythm-playing session man on these recordings).

FINEST MOMENT: Musically, it's probably his cover of Dylan's 'All Along The Watchtower' (exceptional control of bends, consummate tone, beautiful phrasing). However, bluffers would do well to acquaint themselves with his legendary 'Star Spangled Banner' live recording, which uses the guitar to emulate rockets firing, bombs dropping etc. It sounds utterly awful, but of course you must never be seen to admit this.

INSTANT OPINION:
"God came to earth and walked among us for a few short years".

ACCEPTABLE CRITICISM: Possibly, just possibly, you might tentatively suggest that the guitar could just maybe have been slightly out of tune during 'The Star Spangled Banner'?... (HOW DARE YOU MOCK THE MASTER - GET BACK UNDER WHATEVER STONE YOU CRAWLED OUT FROM, YOU REVOLTING PIECE OF WORTHLESS SLIME etc).

Eric Clapton

HISTORY AND BACKGROUND: Born 30th March 1945, Surrey, England. Perhaps the Godfather of all blues bluffers. Influenced (naturally) by **Muddy Waters** and **Robert Johnson**, and was hugely influential himself, not least because of the amount of black blues music that he took to a white rock audience. Joined the **Yardbirds** in 1963, but left quickly, his reason being that their debut single wasn't 'pure blues'. As a result ended up with blues purist **John Mayall**, then left after 15 months to form **Cream** with **Ginger Baker** (drums) and **Jack Bruce** (bass). This was the first blues 'power trio', pre-dating **Hendrix** by more than a year. Outrageous blues-rock guitar antics followed for four albums and numerous US and UK gigs, until the group split in 1968. Formed a succession of 'anonymous' bands, allegedly in an attempt to hide from the guitar-hero label (**Blind Faith**, **Delaney** and **Bonnie**, **Derek & The Dominoes**) although the public always seemed to find out that Eric was behind these within a matter of weeks. Became a solo artist in 1970 and has concentrated on more mellow material ever since.

PLAYING STYLE: They don't call him 'slowhand' for nothing. Since Cream he's calmed down considerably, relying on tone and phrasing to make his long, sustained bent notes carry a platinum-selling tune. He's no mean fingerstyle player either, as demonstrated on the 1992 'MTV Unplugged' album.

TECHNIQUES TO STEAL: Hey, why not play slowly? Slow bends, slow vibrato, slow tempos. The only rapid thing about our Eric is his CD sales. It's also worth trying out playing solos using the neck pickup with just a little overdrive - the resulting 'Woman Tone' is Clapton's blues trademark.

GEAR: Used a Les Paul with the Bluesbreakers, then an SG and 335 with Cream, but arrived in Stratsville in 1970 and has stayed there ever since. First Strat, known as 'Blackie', was retired after 20 years of use; he now plays his own Fender signature model. Used a small Marshall 45 watt combo in Bluesbreaker years; full-tilt Marshall stacks with Cream; now mostly favours Soldano amps.

BLUFFER'S ALBUM: Without a doubt, the album to gain maximum cred with is *John Mayall's Bluesbreakers Featuring Eric Clapton*, known to purists as The Beano album because Eric is shown on the front cover reading the comic. But anyone interested in blues-rock crossover should check out Cream's *Fresh Cream* and *Disraeli Gears*. Some of his solo material is wonderful, but less fashionable than these earlier recordings.

FINEST MOMENT: The solo from the 12-bar-derived epic 'Sunshine Of Your Love' - the first phrase is the main melody from 1950s crooner standard 'Blue Moon', but played with blues timing so it's almost unrecognisable.

INSTANT OPINION: "He's at his best live - never plays a solo the same two nights running."

ACCEPTABLE CRITICISM: Bizarrely, the more success Eric has, and the more sensitive his playing becomes, the more the critics (and the blues trainspotters) want to criticise him. However, you can't beat them, so you might as well join them - pretend that anything post-1970 is 'commercial sell-out' and that his playing's gone downhill since he left the Bluesbreakers.

Stevie Ray Vaughan

HISTORY AND BACKGROUND: Born 3rd October 1954. Younger brother of Jimmie Vaughan, guitarist/vocalist with **The Fabulous Thunderbirds**. Influenced by electric blues players including **BB King**, **Lonnie Mack**, and **Albert Collins**. Formed band 'Double Trouble' in 1981 (the band were named after an **Otis Rush** song) and their demo album *Texas Flood* (recorded in only 3 days) so impressed the record company that it was released without any of the tracks being re-recorded. Three other studio albums followed over the next six years, plus one live recording, each demonstrating the band's obsessive attention to quality control. Luminaries such as **Clapton**, **John Lee Hooker**, and **BB King** admired Stevie Ray's skill and artistry during his lifetime, and he even guested on **David Bowie**'s recording 'Let's Dance' in 1983. The blues world mourned when he was killed in a helicopter crash on August 27th, 1990.

PLAYING STYLE: Extremely fluid up-tempo electric blues, mainly in open-string keys (mainly E, A and B, but de-tuning the whole guitar a semitone). Even his slower tracks featured astonishingly rapid improvising in places. His playing features trills, slides, bends and 'rakes' (skimming across one or more strings before picking the note), and gives more than a cursory nod to Hendrix.

TECHNIQUES TO STEAL: In a word - legato. Use hammer-ons and pull-offs like you're on a commission for every one you play. You might like to throw in some wide vibrato and plenty of 'static' bends (bend up one string, then hold the bend while you play a different note on the next string). Also, try switching pickups every 16 bars or so during a solo.

GEAR: Various Strats, including a famous early '60s model nicknamed 'Lenny', with which he recorded the instrumental of the same name. Started mainly using Fender Vibroverb amps, though in later years began to favour Dumble heads and even Marshalls.

BLUFFER'S ALBUM: You might want to start with the band's debut *Texas Flood*. As there are only four albums, you should really have all of them, and besides, it's bluffing suicide if all you have is an SRV greatest hits compilation.

FINEST MOMENT: In true blues referential style, some of his greatest playing occurs on the band's instrumental cover version of Hendrix's 'Little Wing', but the open-string licks in 'Pride And Joy' are exemplary.

INSTANT OPINION (stolen from John Lee Hooker): **"He was one of the greatest musicians who ever lived, and it was a great loss to the world, to the blues, and to me."**

ACCEPTABLE CRITICISM: Poor choice of inter-gig transport.

Emergency backup bluffs

Here are some bluffing basics on a further four players, just in case you need additional reference to prove your depth of knowledge.

1. Kenny-Wayne Shepherd

Included because he's the newest guitarist on the scene – mentioning KWS can guarantee instant cred with younger blues dudes. Strat player, and the youngest Fender endorsee to have his own guitar designed for him.

Debut album 'Ledbetter Heights' launched onto a largely desolate US blues market. **SRV** inspired Kenny to play blues, but like many a good bluffer, he sensibly now cites the obligatory **Muddy Waters, Albert Collins, Howlin' Wolf** etc. as influences.

2. Freddie King

Influential Texan electric blues player - bridges gap between **Howlin' Wolf/Muddy Waters** era of the 40s/50s and electric blues explosion of mid-60s. Gibson semi-solid player - used ES-335s, ES-345s and ES-355s. Used plastic thumbpick and steel fingerpick to pick out melodies.

Early user of distorted tone. Some players may know his 1970s recordings, on which **Clapton** guested. Brave bluffers should fearlessly compare these unfavourably with his '50s and '60s material, including the singles 'Hideaway' and 'Lonesome Whistle Blues'.

3. Blind Lemon Jefferson

Blues pioneer - essential to know if you're going to outbluff a **Robert Johnson** fan. Made his first blues recording 1925 – i.e. earlier than almost anyone else – and died four years later. Played acoustic fingerstyle, using alternating thumb technique, creating mix of gospel, blues and country.

Had a chauffeur who drove him everywhere because he was genuinely blind (that's Blind Lemon who was genuinely blind, not the chauffeur). Hits included 'Pneumonia Blues', 'Black Snake Blues' and 'Matchbox Blues' (covered by **Carl Perkins** whose version was, in turn, covered by The Beatles).

Mysteriously, no guitarist ever seems to own any Blind Lemon Jefferson recordings, so you can usually talk knowledgeably about tone, feel and technique without fear of contradiction.

4. Peter Green

The most arcane of the UK blues-rock players. Started well, even showing signs of embryonic bluffing skills by name-checking **Freddie** and **BB King** as influences.

Joined **John Mayall**'s Bluesbreakers in 1966, replacing the departed **Clapton**. Left Bluesbreakers (leaving a space for a young **Mick Taylor**, later of **Rolling Stones** fame) to form **Fleetwood Mac**, recording classic singles such as 'Oh Well' and 'Albatross'. Disappeared due to drug and mental health problems for a decade or so, resurfacing briefly in the early 1980s to produce relatively unsuccessful albums, then re-appeared in 1996 to record 'The Peter Green Splinter Group Album'.

Mainly a Strat player, but has been seen with Gibsons too. Known for excellent intonation, consummate vibrato and intuitive phrase construction (or, put in bluffer terms, 'amazing feel', 'God-given touch', and 'the talent to make that piece of wood sing'.)

It's Easy To Bluff... Music and TAB Guide

Most guitar players can't read music. There. We've said it. So you can stop feeling guilty about it and get on with the serious business of pretending that you can. On these two pages you'll find tab and treble clef notation for all of the techniques featured in this book, along with tips on how to play them.

HOW TO READ TREBLE CLEF: The note on the bottom line of the treble clef is middle E – that is, it's the E which is found on the 2nd fret of the D string. The top line is F (1st fret, high E string).

Guitar notes that are lower or higher than this range are notated using 'leger lines' – these are extra stave lines drawn in above or below the main clef.

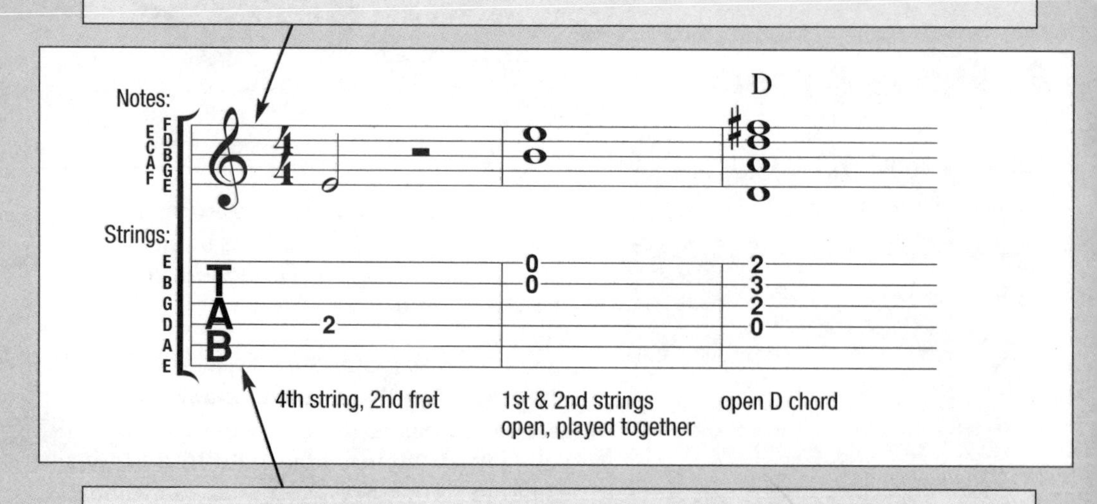

HOW TO READ TAB: The six lines represent the strings – the thickest (lowest) string is at the bottom. The number shows the fret.

HOW TO READ CHORD PARTS: The chord names are written above, and sometimes the musical rhythm of the part is notated underneath.

If no rhythm is given, or you see several even 'slashes' in a bar, then normally you should make up your own rhythm pattern. If you see two chords in a bar, it's normally assumed that they're played for two beats each.

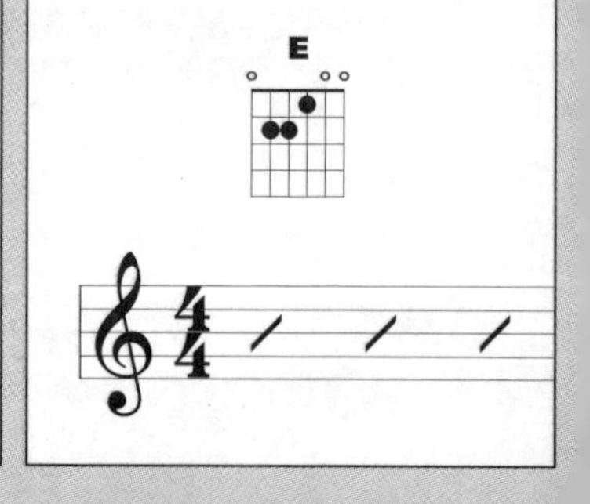

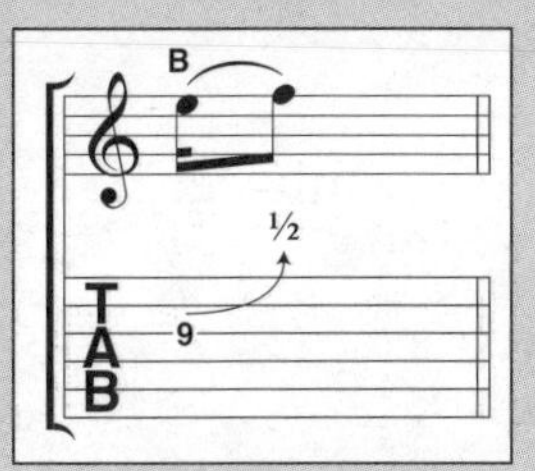

SEMITONE BEND (OR HALF-STEP BEND): Play the note with the picking hand then bend it up a semitone (so it reaches the pitch of the note on the next fret).

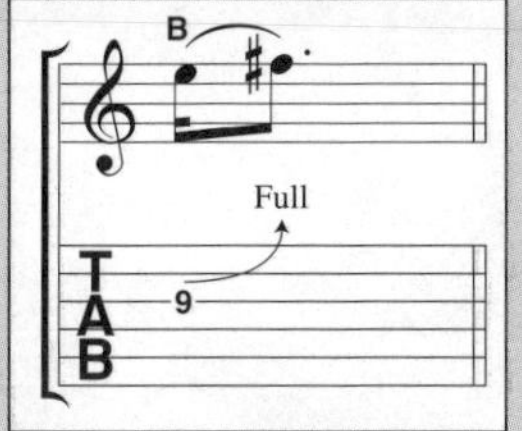

WHOLE TONE BEND: Duh! Just bend it further!

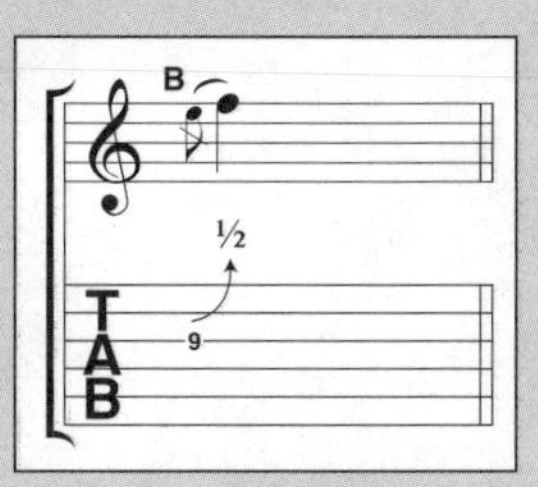

GRACE NOTE BEND: The only difference with these is that you start bending as soon as you've picked the note. You should hardly hear the first note.

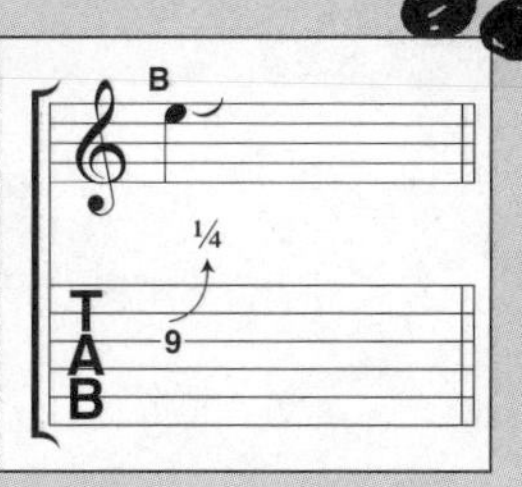

QUARTER-TONE BEND: Just bend the string a little – don't go as far as a semitone. Quarter-tone is used to mean any bend that's less than a semitone.

BEND AND RELEASE: Play the note, bend it up, let it back down again.

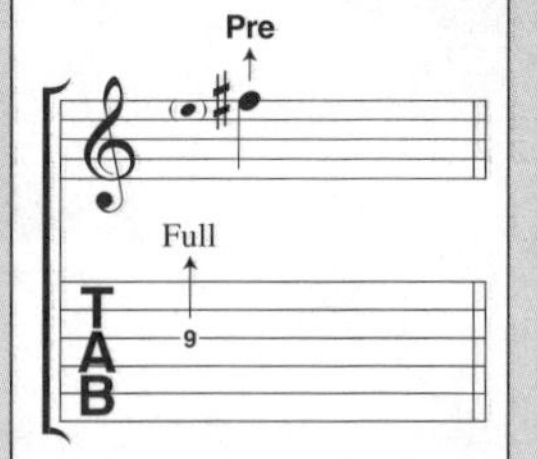

PRE-BEND: Bend the note up before you play it.

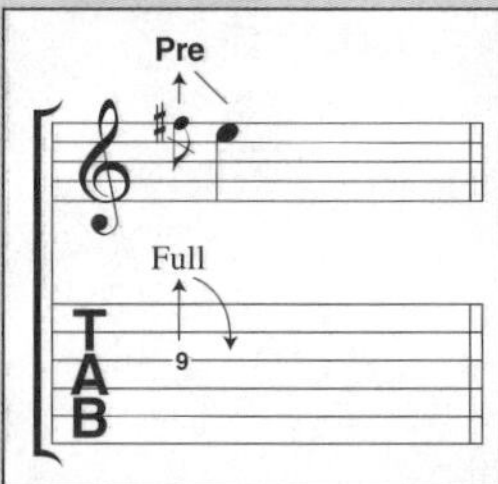

PRE-BEND AND RELEASE: Bend the note up, then play it, then release the bend while the note rings on.

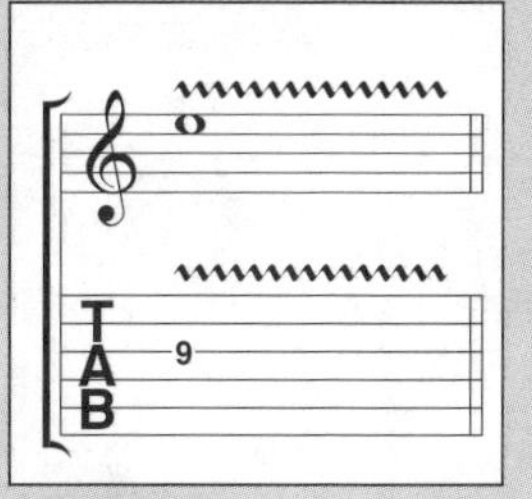

VIBRATO: Move the string up and down by rapidly bending and releasing it by a small amount.

HAMMER-ON: Pick one note, then sound the higher note by fretting it without re-picking. Hammer-ons are always ascending in pitch.

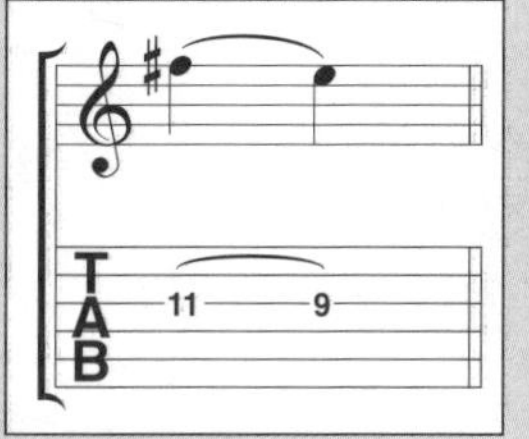

PULL-OFF: Get both fingers into the positions shown in the tab, then pick the higher note. Whilst it rings on, pull the finger off the string to sound the lower note.

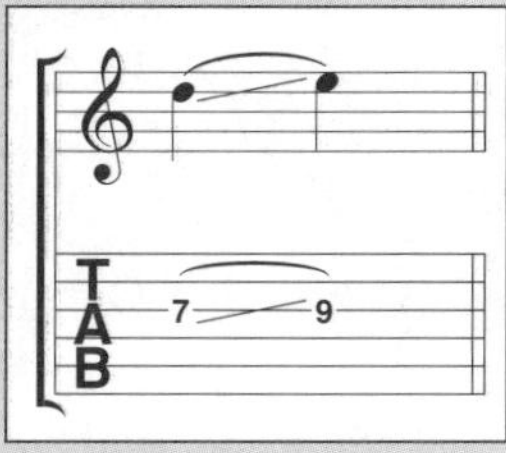

SLIDE/GLISS: While the note is sounding, slide the fretting finger up or down to the position shown in the tab.

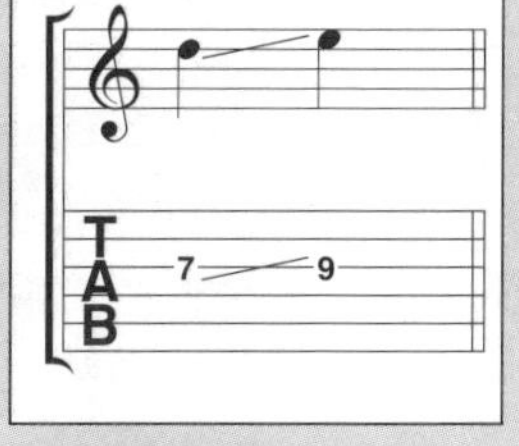

SLIDE/GLISS AND RESTRIKE: As before, but this time repick the second note after you've finishing sliding.

TAPPING: Fret the note using the picking hand by tapping onto the position shown. Usually followed by a pull-off.

PALM MUTING: Rest the picking hand on the strings very near to the bridge. This partially mutes the notes – the technique is used a lot in blues and rock rhythm playing.

SLASH CHORDS: Many players get confused when they see chord notation like this for the first time. Do not fear – it's simple. The letter name before the slash is the chord you play. The one after the slash is the bass note. Bluffing tip - if you find it too difficult to play a particular bass note at the same time as the chord, try ignoring it and just playing the chord, then get a bassist or keyboard player to supply the bottom end.

Willie Dixon's 'Little Red Rooster' was covered by blues disciples the **Rolling Stones** in 1964.

Rhythm patterns or 'Flash don't make cash'

If you have to bluff your way through a whole blues gig, you'll need to convince everyone in the band that you know your 'blues chops', so it's vital that you can play some basic accompaniment styles. In this section you'll find 10 rhythm and picking patterns, in progressive order of difficulty, which blues guitarists use when accompanying vocalists or other soloists.

Rhythm Tips

- Most electric blues players use a pick rather than fingers for rhythm work. And if you're playing in 4/4 time, you should generally favour downstrokes rather than upstrokes.
- **Avoid piling on too much distortion because the chords will lose definition...**
- ...but don't have the sound too clean either. Most blues strum-merchants try to recreate the sound of a *slightly* overdriven amp (mainly so they can use bluff-friendly words like 'bite', 'crunch', 'edge' and 'meat').
- **Straight major chords can almost always be improved by replacing them with 7th chords...**
- ...and try replacing straight minor chords with minor 7ths. Instant jazz-blues!
- **If you're playing an acoustic, ditch that £1000-plus Taylor or vintage Martin that plays like a dream. Get a cheap piece of Korean-made nastiness with two-year-old strings and a balsa wood body. In many cases, you'll find that acoustic Delta blues actually sounds more authentic on cheap guitars.**
- If you're using a cheap electric guitar with an action like an egg-slicer, simply tune it to an open G chord (DGDGBD) and get yourself a bottleneck. A high action is actually an advantage for slide players.
- **Don't strum all of the strings, all of the time. Blues accompaniment is often extremely sparse, and usually concentrates on the bass strings of the instrument.**
- Strat players - don't set the treble on the amplifier too high, and avoid the bridge pickup at all costs. You don't want your accompaniment to slice through a mix as, say, a funk player might. Most of the time, you should be after a more middly tone.
- **Try playing slightly 'behind the beat' (i.e. make sure some of the strums occur a fraction of a second 'late'). This will help to give your playing a naturally laid-back feel, and also help to combat the natural tendency of most inexperienced guitarists to speed up throughout a song.**

No Sweat Rooster

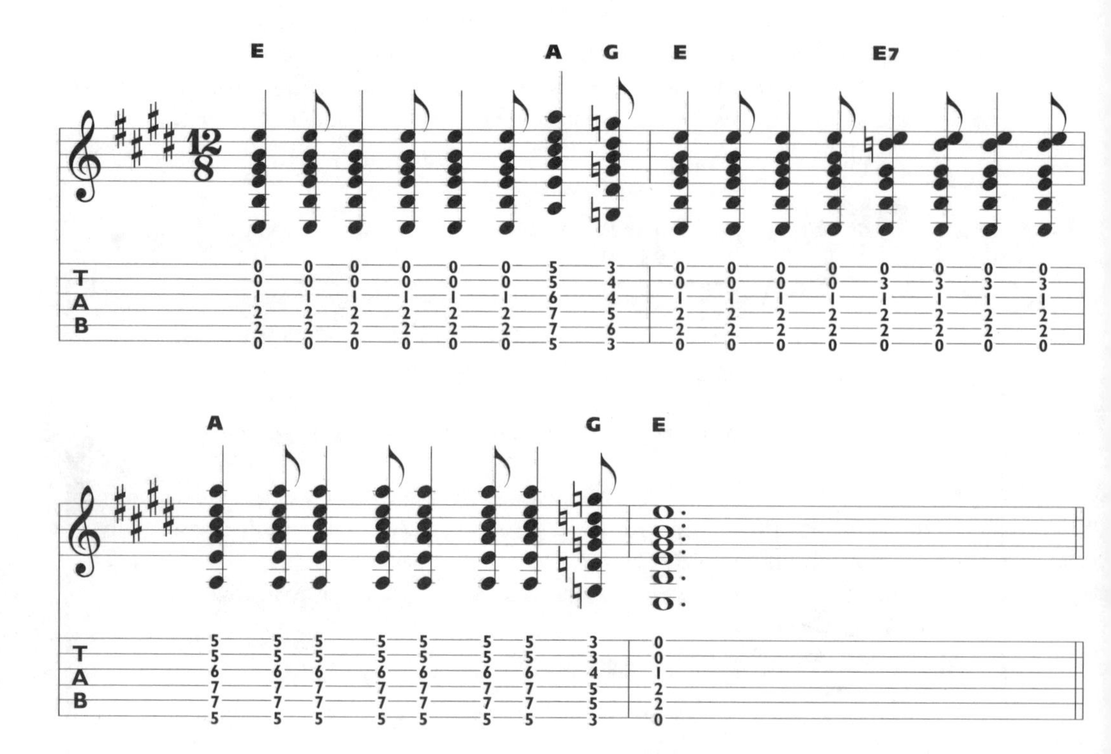

This moody 'Little Red Rooster' style figure should be played at a relaxed tempo. In any case, it would be difficult to play quickly without compromising the feel and/or your image as a laid back blues player.

In an emergency, you could make life easier by covering the changes using open strings for the first/last beat of each chord. **Don't let anyone catch you sweating!**

Time To Bluff

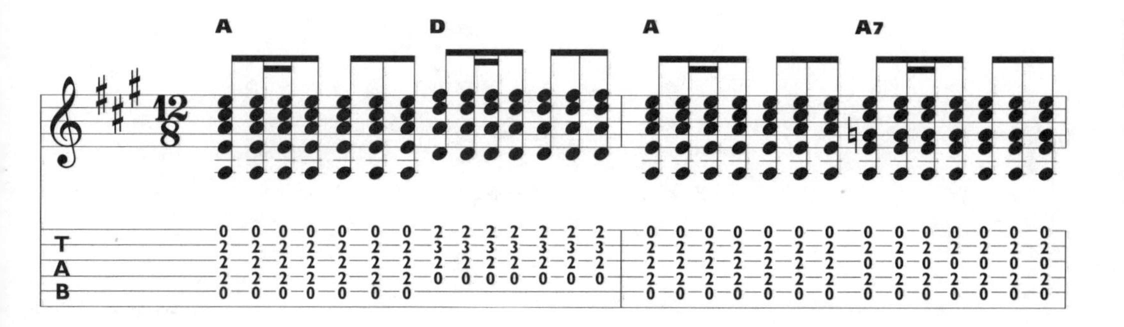

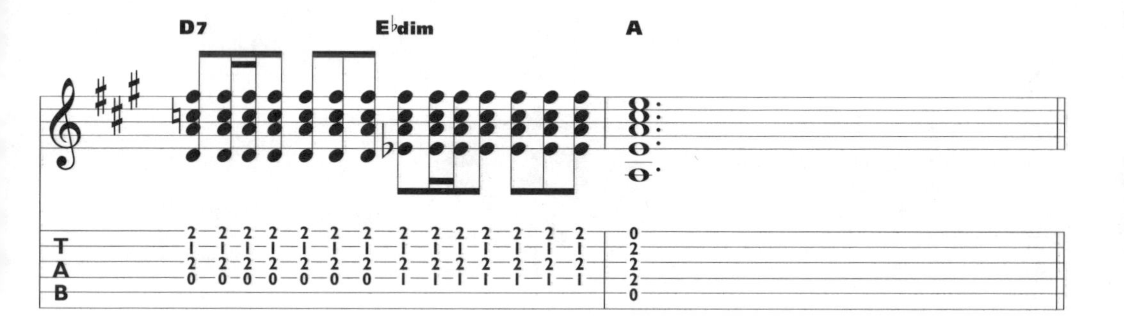

A bluffer's dream! All that strumming makes it easy to keep track of the beat and camouflages chord changes beautifully. To make life easier still, try lifting each chord off on the last quaver beat, giving you longer to find the next chord while the open strings ring. And no matter how good it sounds, remember to look a little bit bored.

Bluffing From Birth

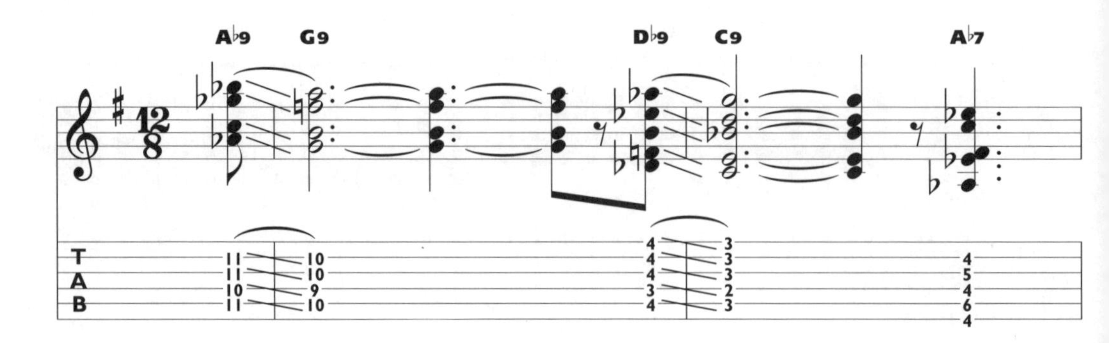

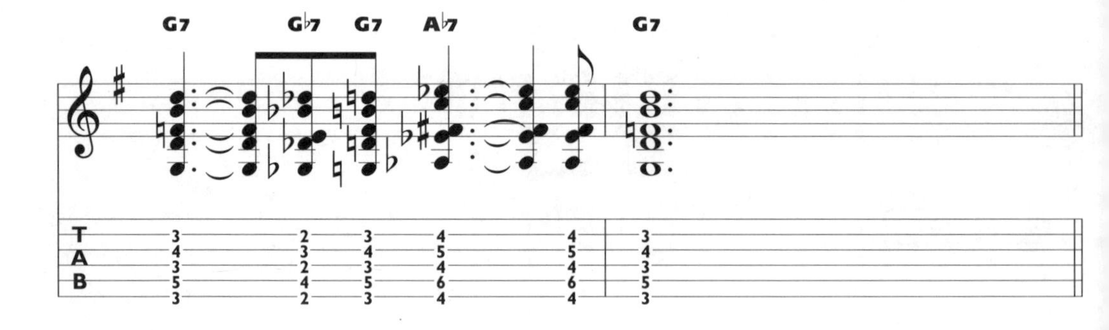

Spice up an otherwise static rhythm pattern with a dose of chromaticism. **It could turn your standard blues licks into a religious experience!**

This simple movement of chords a semitone at a time will convince all but the most hardened bluffer that you have been playing the blues in smoky bars since before they were born.

Smokestack Shuffle

This groove is reminiscent of **Hubert Sumlin**'s 'Smokestack Lightnin' and it features everything that's cool about an unaccompanied blues riff; lazy shuffle beat, muted rhythm accents and a hint of pentatonic scale.

This makes it an ideal candidate for carelessly reeling off as if it were second nature while tuning up - if you work on it at home first!

Freddie In A Felt Hat

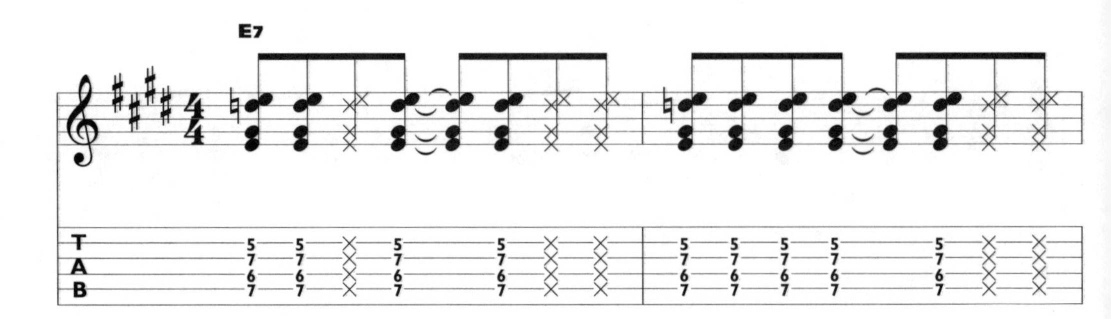

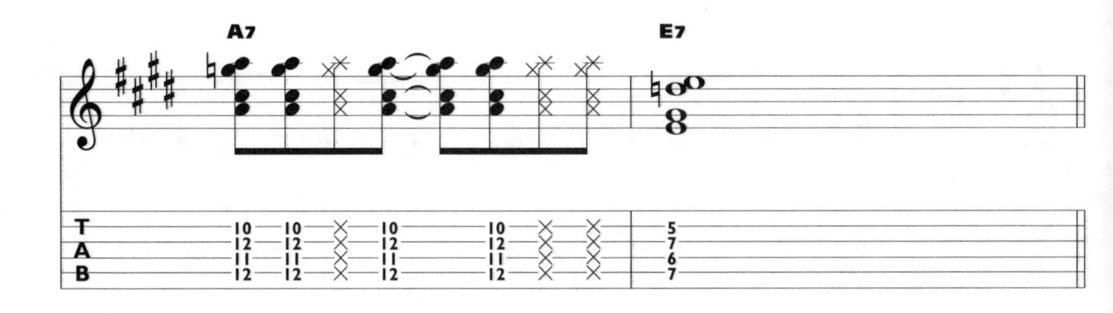

This relaxed accompaniment style was very popular in the '60s when it was used by artists like **Freddie King** and **The Rolling Stones**.

Don't blow your cred by getting too busy with the strumming. It's okay for your hat to fall over your eyes, but you don't want to risk it falling on the floor...

Classic Backbeat

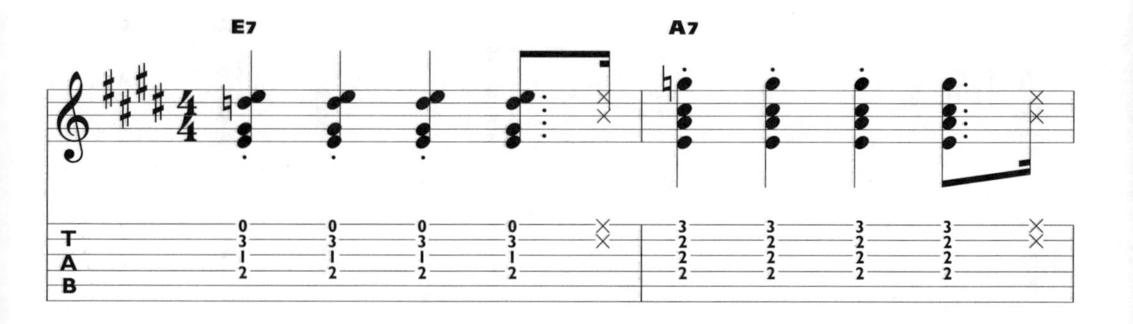

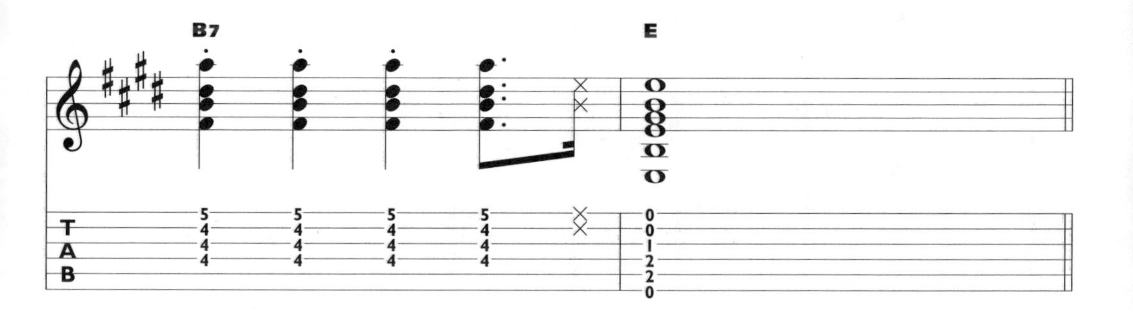

What could be a very 'straight' sounding rhythm pattern is given a blues lilt by adding a muted upstroke at the end of each bar. This also makes the rhythm less exposed and easier to articulate.

Feel free to vary this by adding off-beats or accents, but don't lose sight of the raw simplicity - **make each variation count!**

Spirit Of Jangle

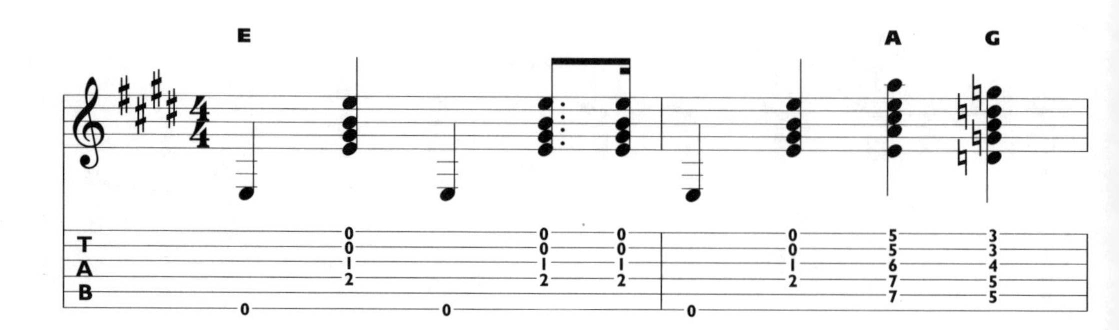

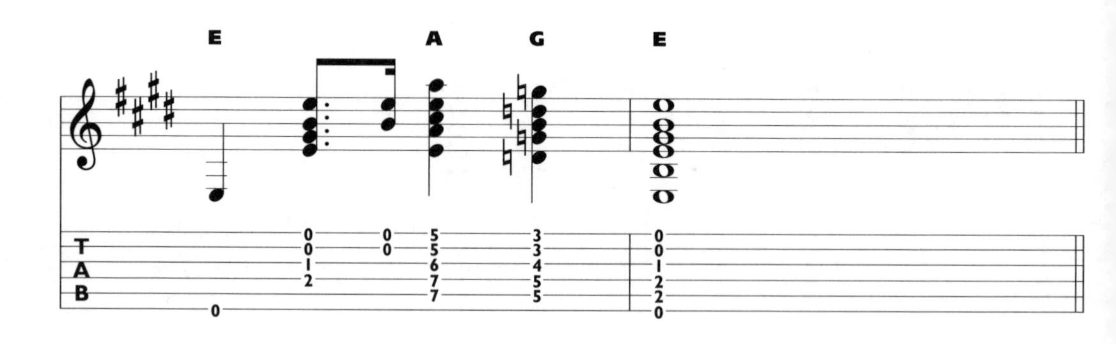

For a brighter, more 'jangly' type of blues rhythm, this strumming style is ideal. Try mixing it with some of the other more subdued patterns to give your rhythm playing more dynamic variation.

Remember, if your rhythm playing is good, people don't seem to mind you taking longer solos.

Shuff That Bluffle

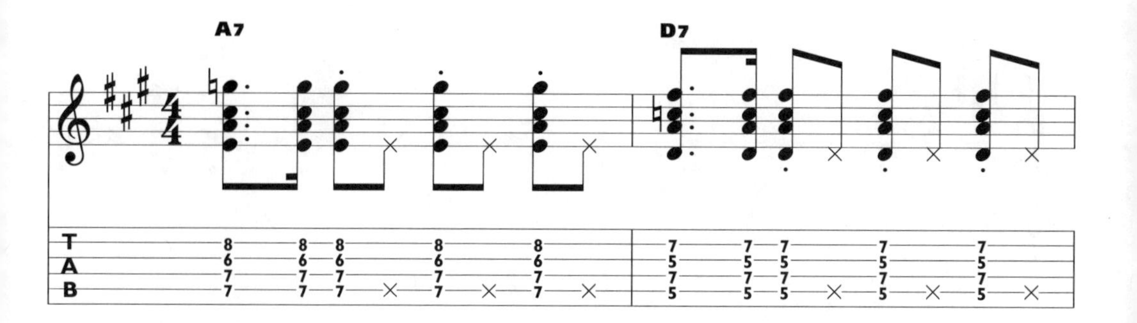

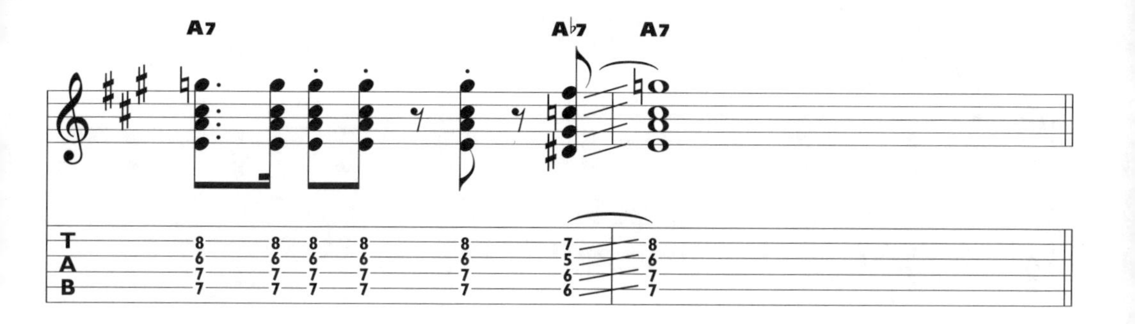

When an **R&B feel** is required, it's amazing how lost some players seem when they need to be rhythmic yet sparse. Stand out from the crowd with this simple but tricky-sounding pattern.

Take care to mute unwanted open strings, and exaggerate the **staccato feel**, but remember - this should look effortless.

Everybody Needs Sunglasses

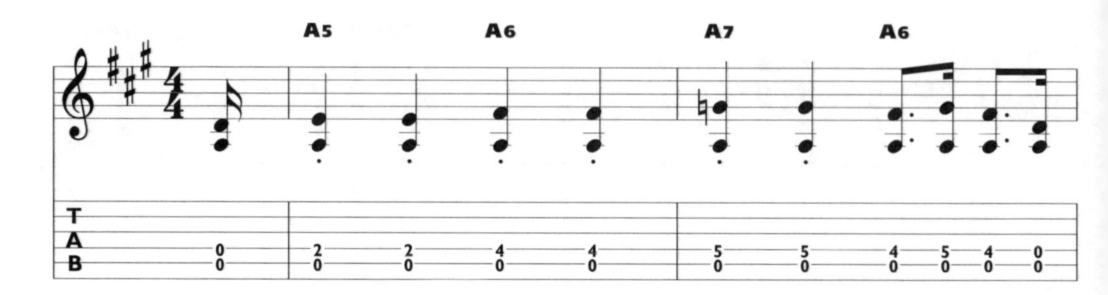

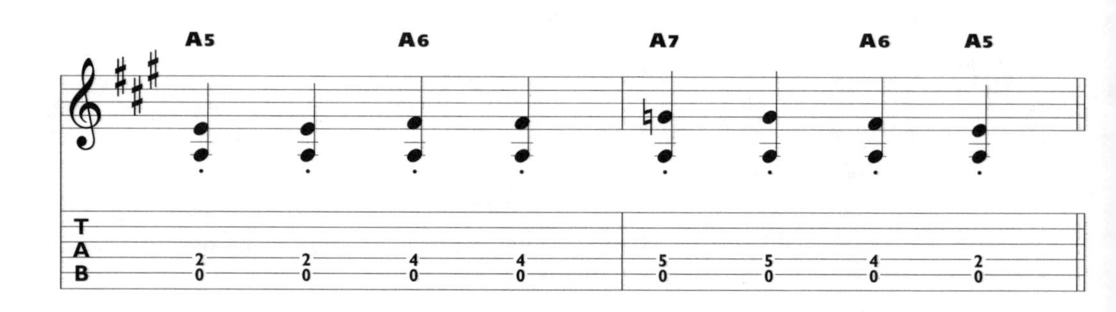

Just the thing to play when you are wearing those '**Blues Brothers**' shades. Try adding a hint of distortion for a more menacing Stones-type feel. This pattern can be moved along a string to transpose to D, or back a string to E, making a ready-made 12-bar which you can use at any jam session.

Moore Of Rory

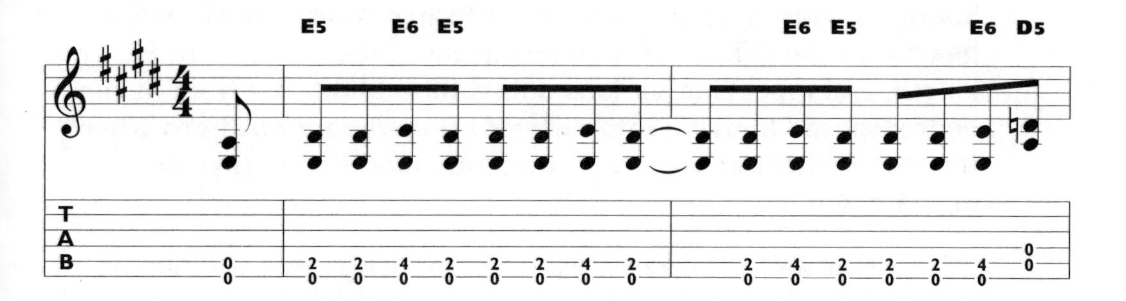

This hard-edged blues riff wouldn't sound out of place under a searing **Rory Gallagher** solo. Give it a swing feel and it also conjures up images of **Gary Moore**.

When a song's rhythm part is as upfront as this, you should keep the accompaniment exactly as written, **then go wild on the solo!**

Blues Riffs or 'Play it over and over until it sounds good'

Blues, perhaps more than any other form of guitar music, relies heavily on the riff. A riff is almost always one, two or four bars in length, and repeats at various points throughout the track. It can be transposed (moving into different fingerboard positions when the chords change) or it may be slightly modified to take account of the changes.

In this section, we've also included blues 'licks'. A lick is a lead guitar part that you learn beforehand, and then include as part of an so-called 'improvised' solo. It follows that licks are, of course, vital to a bluffer's defensive equipment, because they can be inserted in a lead part without anyone knowing that you prepared them before the gig.

The difference between a **riff** and a **lick** is basically that you may only use a **lick** once (pretending it's a great phrase you just thought up) but you can use a **riff** over and over, demonstrating how you can make one simple idea into a whole musical experience by the power of your touch, feel and tone (man.)

In this section you'll find 24 riffs of varying levels of difficulty, together with tips and suggestions about when - and when not - to use them. If you're a complete beginner on guitar, don't be afraid to concentrate purely on the easy examples - other players will admire your sense of cool restraint.

Quarter Commitment

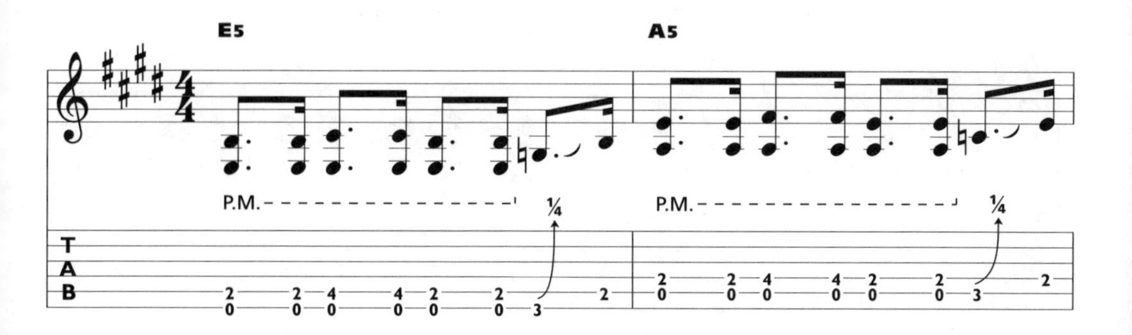

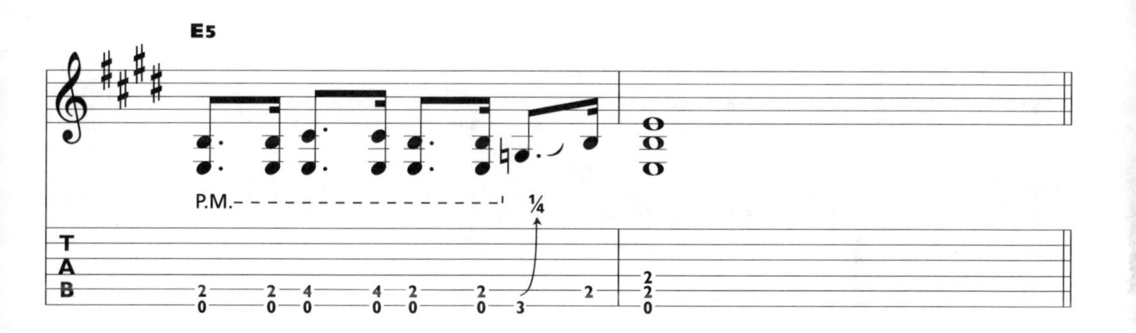

This Bring It On Home-style playing works best with the neck pickup selected and the tone on about half. The partial palm muting means almost no hand movement is visible, which looks much more impressive to a blues audience. Don't underestimate the importance of those quarter tone bends either. **They play an essential part in the bluffer's art of refusing to commit to major or minor!**

Any Time Now

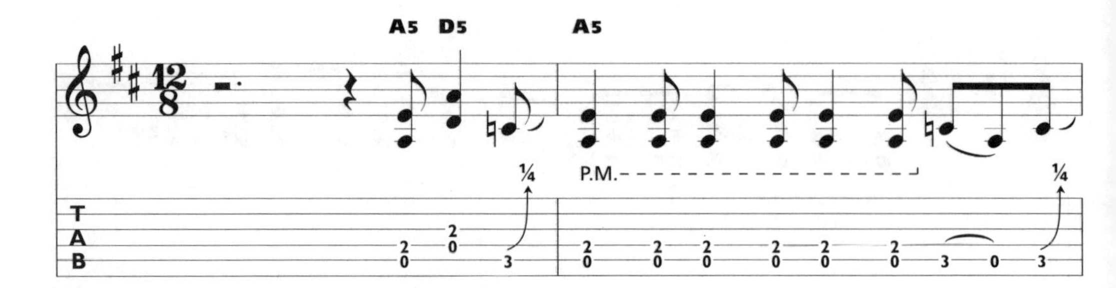

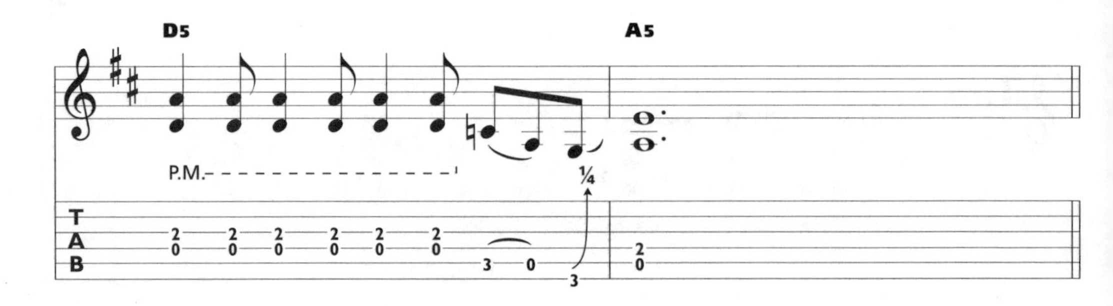

Settle into a menacing pulse with this solid accompaniment riff, which just hints at the fact that you could launch into a wailing solo at any moment! The quarter tone bends and pull-offs will gain further credibility if you don't try to make them too perfect.

Warning

The occasional sharp note or string rattle is expected of you, so don't blow your cover by being too rehearsed.

Bob's Dawg

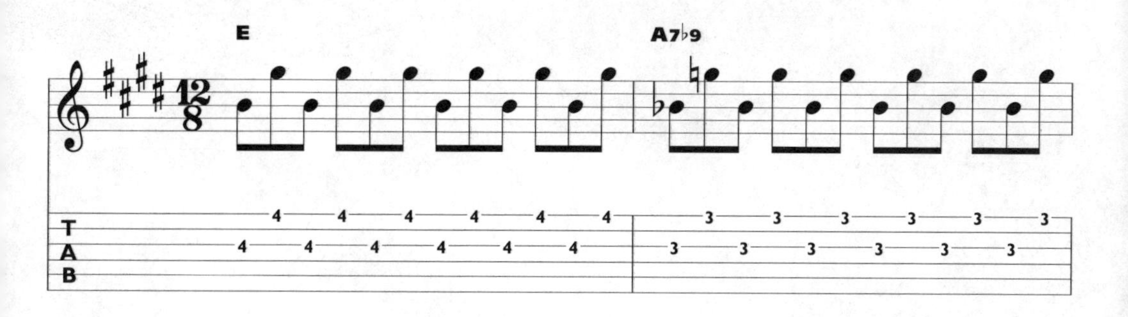

Here's an opportunity to show off a little of your authentic Robert Johnson fingerpicking technique. Add vibrato from the fretting hand and the band will follow you into a 12 bar sequence in a key of your choice. Slide up into bars 1 and 3 to show your audience what it means to play with **authority**.

Many of **Jimmy Page**'s classic rock riffs with Led Zeppelin were based on blues ideas - he just played them a little louder than most people...

Passport To Bluffsville

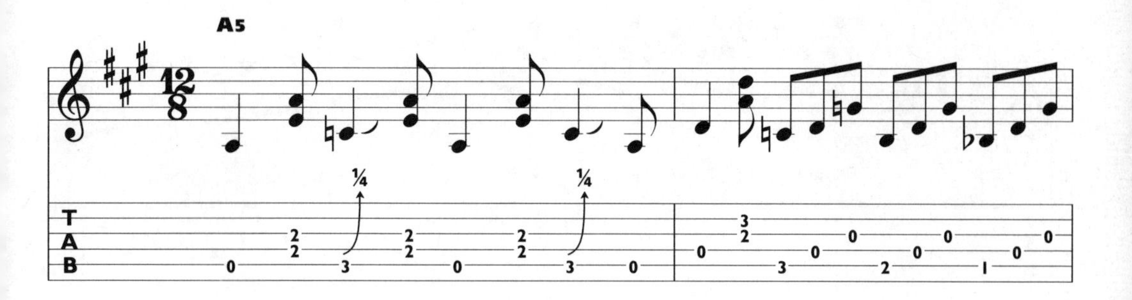

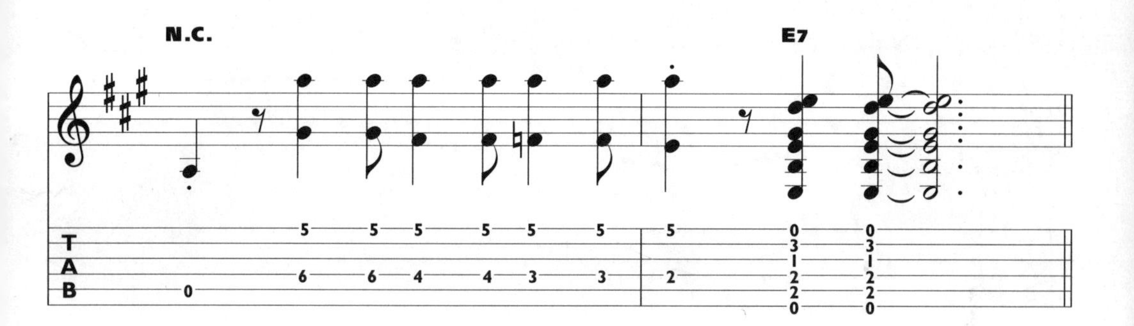

There's no way anyone will ever doubt your blues credentials if you slip this turnaround idea in at the conclusion of a solo.
If you replace the E7 in the fourth bar with an A7, **you have the perfect ending too!**

I'm Still Here, Man

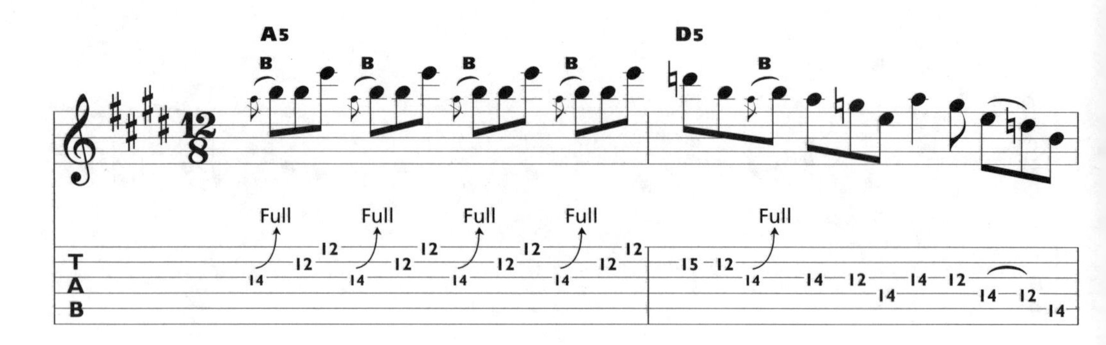

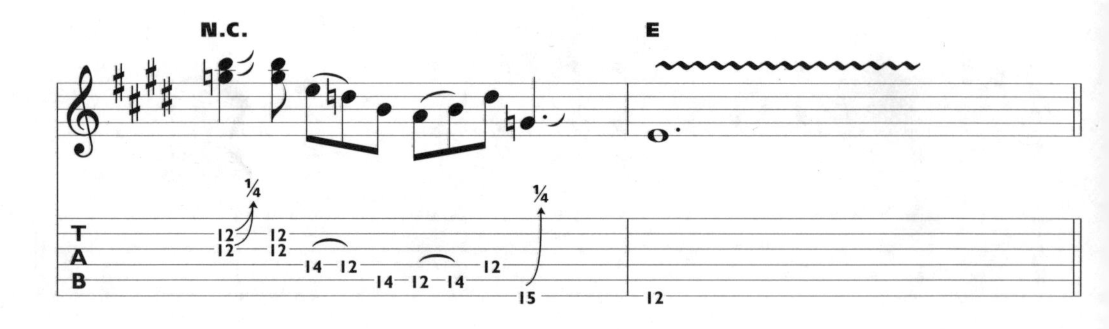

When you feel it's time to make your presence felt a little more; i.e., **after a flashy sax/harmonica break**, employ this repetitive device at the beginning of your solo, to show you won't be left in the dust.

Don't let any concern about this show in your face - perhaps frown and nod a little as you let it fly.

Bluffaway

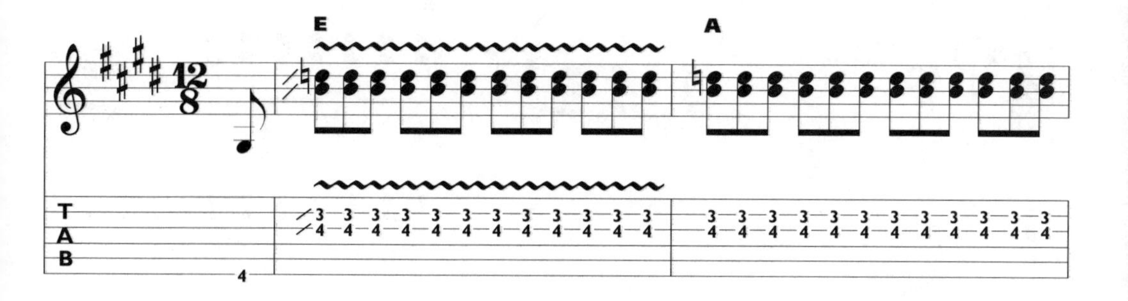

This riff works really well unaccompanied, making it ideal as an intro or as part of a solo, while the band just play chord accents. It should be played with a little vibrato and lot of attitude!

If asked, you should say that your slightly overdriven tone is influenced by **Eric Clapton**'s Les Paul/ Marshall sound on 'Hideaway' from the *Bluesbreakers* album (which you have on vinyl of course).

Albert's Sweet Kansas Home

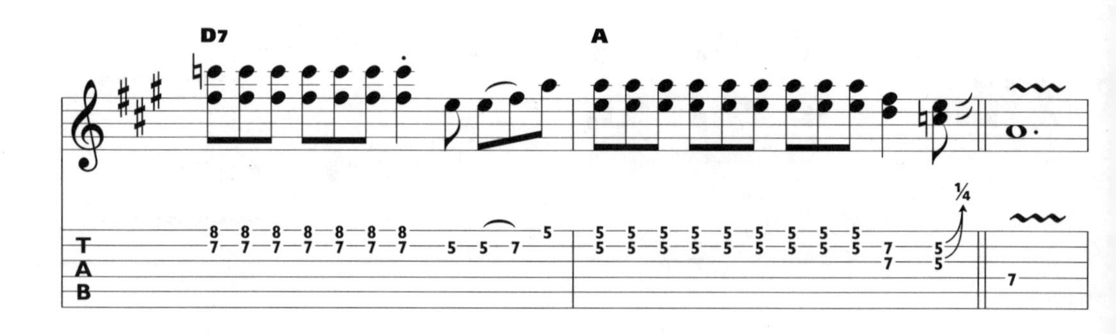

Once again, here is an ideal intro/solo phrase, with a hint of '50s Rock'n'Roll in those double stops. This would really cut a dash with a razor-sharp **Albert Collins** style tone.

Though it's quite aggressive, you'll find it ideal for reeling off casually, while the band put all their effort into those chord stabs!

Cool Stops

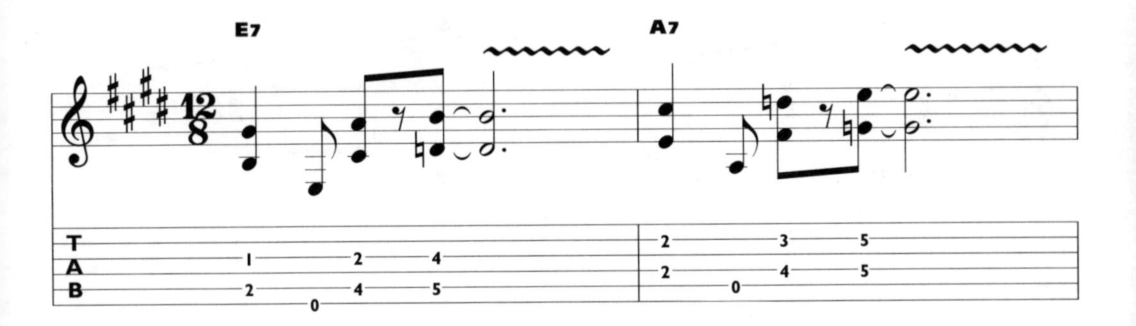

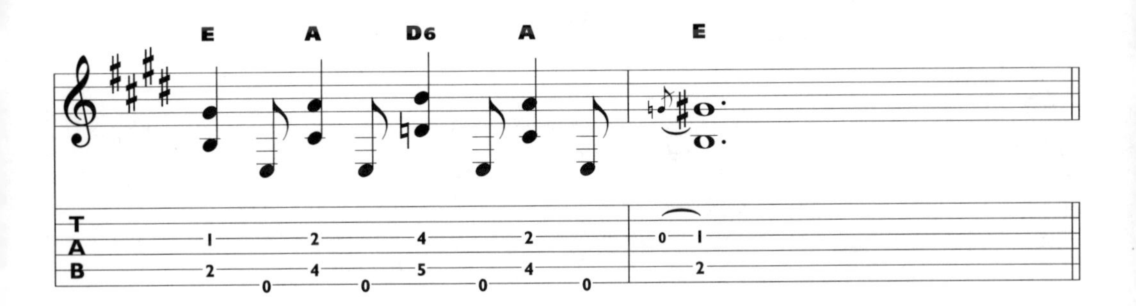

Using this figure creatively, it should be fairly easy to put together a great laid back blues backing that sounds full and interesting, without ever using a complete chord.

Perhaps a couple of choruses would benefit from being played in the busier style demonstrated in bar 3, then reverting to the sparser part, to add dynamics and generally be more impressive.

Know Your Onions

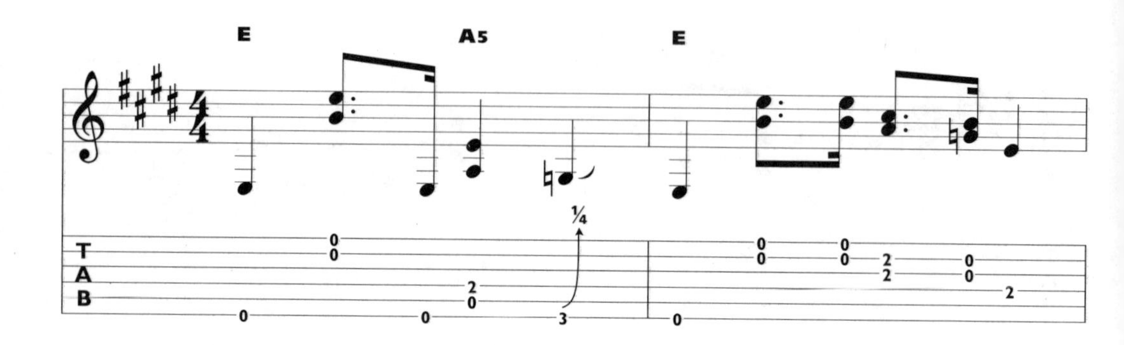

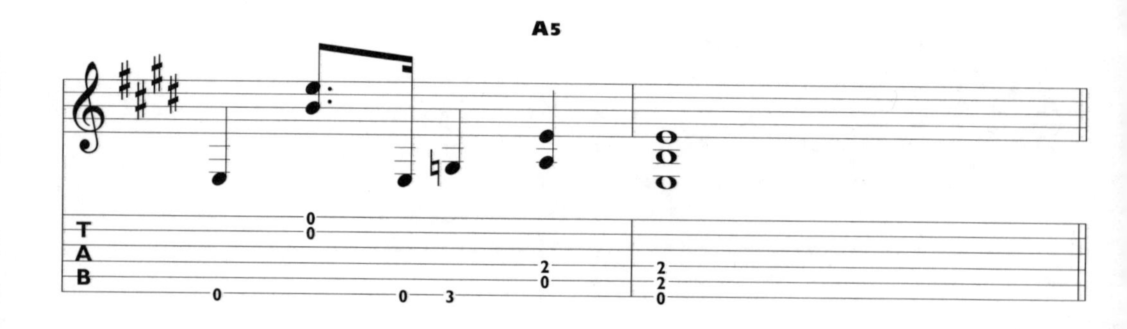

Depending on how you choose to approach it, this pattern can be up tempo and driving, maybe with a little natural sounding amp distortion, or slow and forlorn with the tone backed off on the neck pickup. Either way, keep it from sounding too full by avoiding whole chords - **don't play any more than two strings simultaneously.**

Almost A Solo

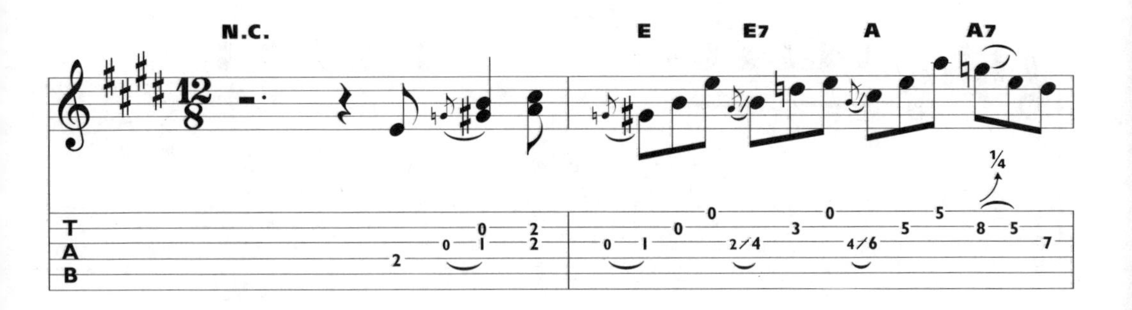

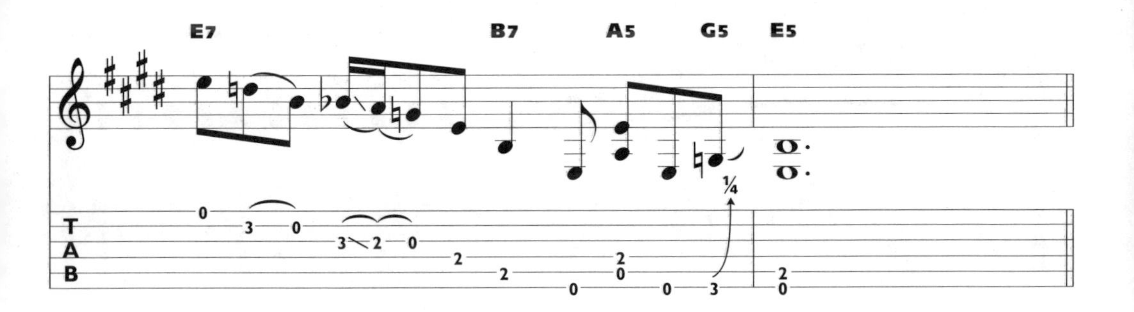

This figure is easier to play than it sounds, making it ideal for when you need to pull something special out of the bag, while maintaining the correct blues demeanour. The quarter tone bend in bar 2 breaks the usual precedent by pulling the string down to facilitate an easier pull-off. The shift back down to open position keeps this riff out of 'solo' territory.

Acoustic Delta

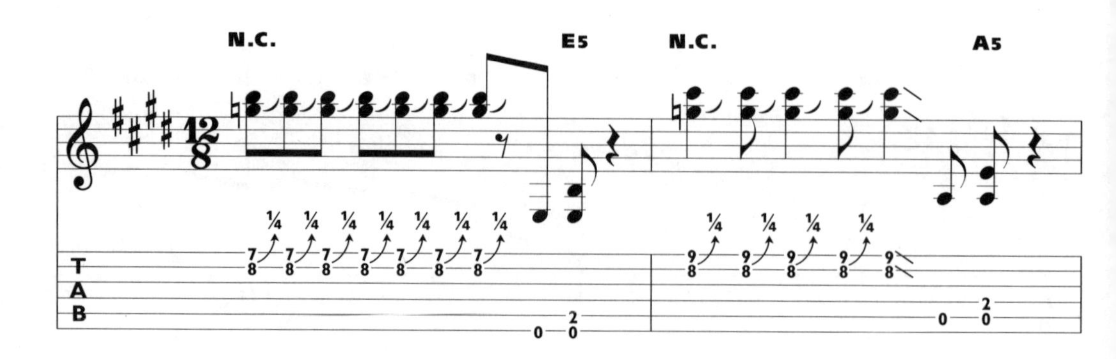

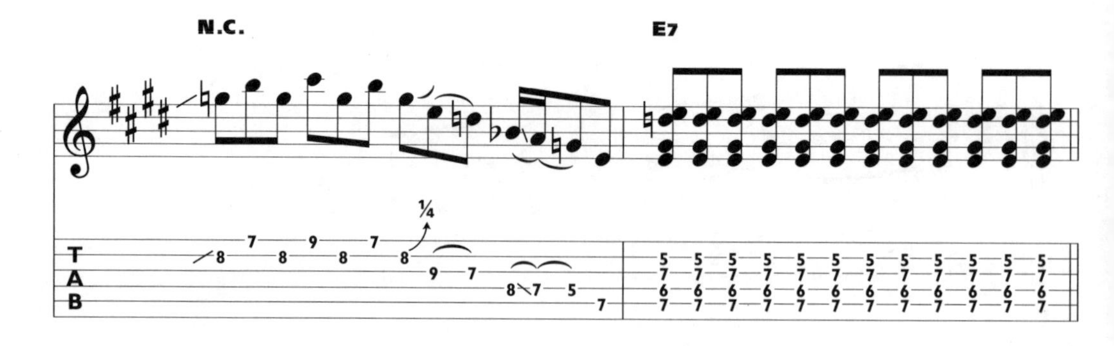

Play this one when you're trying out acoustic guitars in the music shop.

It makes a real feature of the ever-present quarter-tone bend. Try not to bend the first string or some of the effect is lost. Of course, the chord stabs might not seem so necessary with a bass player and drummer to lend a hand, but they do add punch and make it look as if you are leading the band.

Stevie's Soundcheck

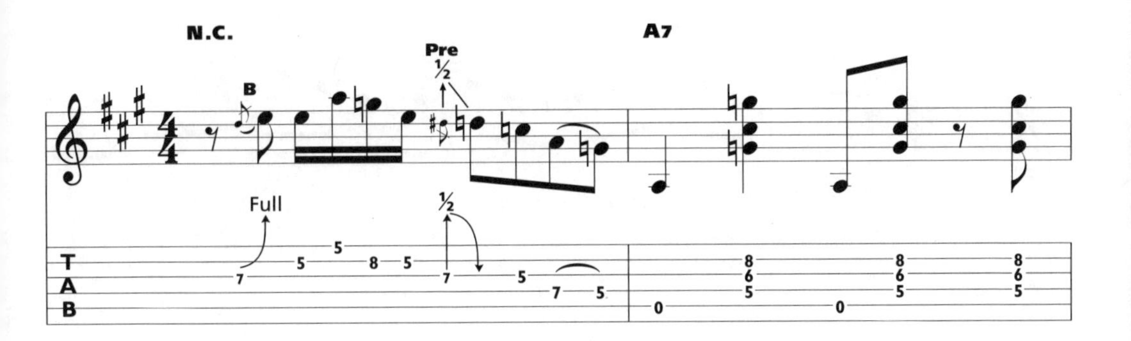

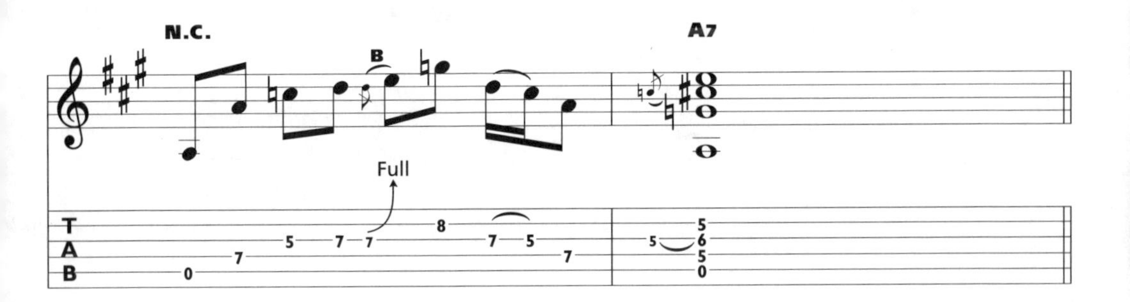

This **SRV**-style workout allows you to show that you can cover all bases without any need for a rhythm guitarist, who might easily dilute your credibility.

Note the use of open strings to fill out the chordal segments, making this a great soundcheck/tuning up showcase, as it will stand up on its own.

Do, however, remember to keep it brief and leave 'em wanting more!

Fast And Cool

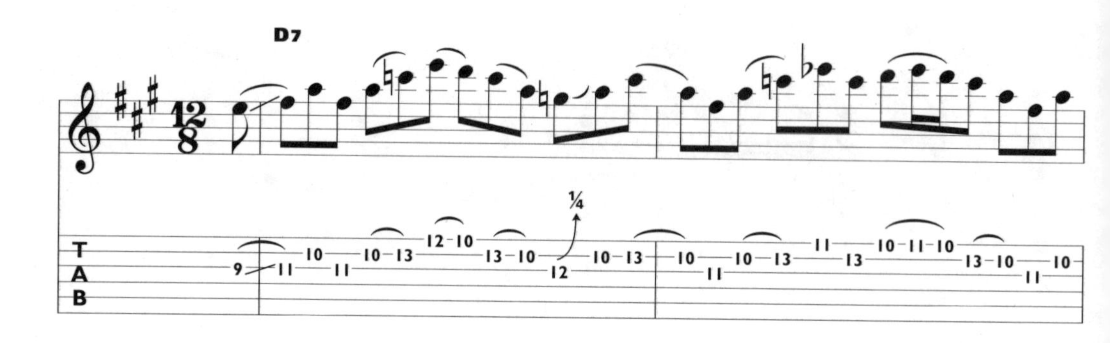

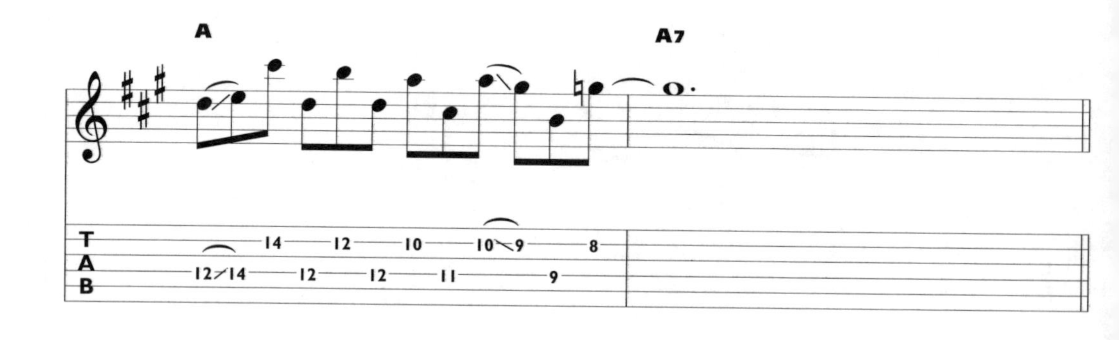

Although it's not all that fast, this is an undeniably fiddly-sounding solo lick, and is moveable to a variety of keys around the fretboard. The intervals in bar 3 will probably be easier to articulate at speed using pick and fingers. Because there is quite a lot happening in a short space of time, this is recommended for more up-tempo numbers (it also makes any fluffed notes less noticeable).

Fast And Hot But Still Cool

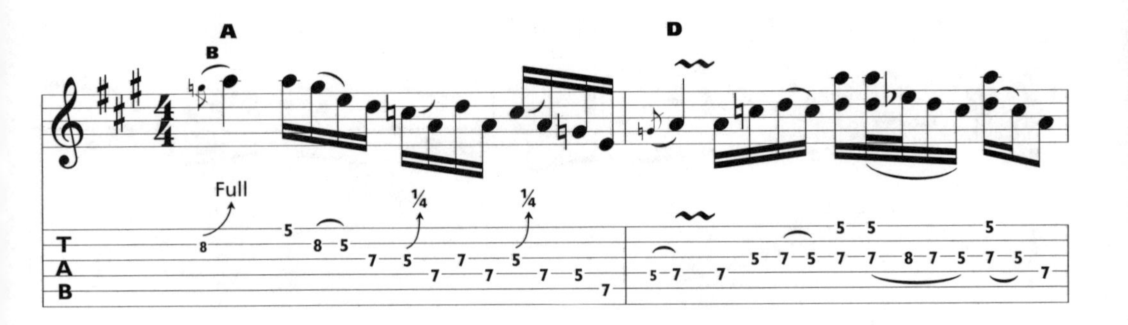

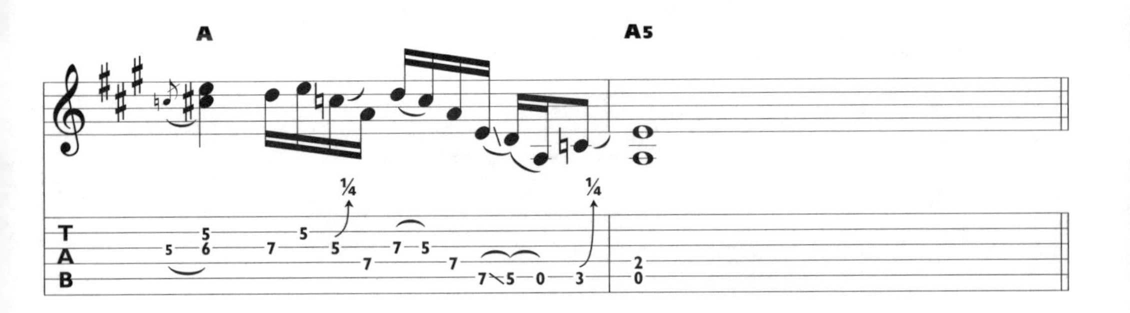

Crotchet arco on the downbeat, followed by semiquaver groups featuring diads - or, put another way, long notes and short notes in the same riff! The phrase mixes traditional double-stops with a '**Clapton-esque**' single note approach.

Needless to say, you will of course mention that the roots of this mixture can be traced back to **Robert Johnson** and **Charley Patton**.

Rehearsed Improv

Hendrix Tip

This concentrated example of **Hendrix-style** double stops doesn't need to be played with pick and fingers technique.

It sounds better using a hard picking attack with a relatively clean tone. Don't try to be too tidy with your execution - rehearse it over and over again until it sounds spontaneous.

Bottle Bluffing

Taking a few traditional influences on board, this phrase begins with the classic quarter tone bend sequence that shows your blues pedigree from the start.

During the second bar, the slides are voiced to subtly imitate the sound of a bottleneck (a trick used by **Jeff Beck**) without all the hassle of actually using one. It winds up with a cool slide/pull-off sequence down the E blues scale.

Taste-Free Zone

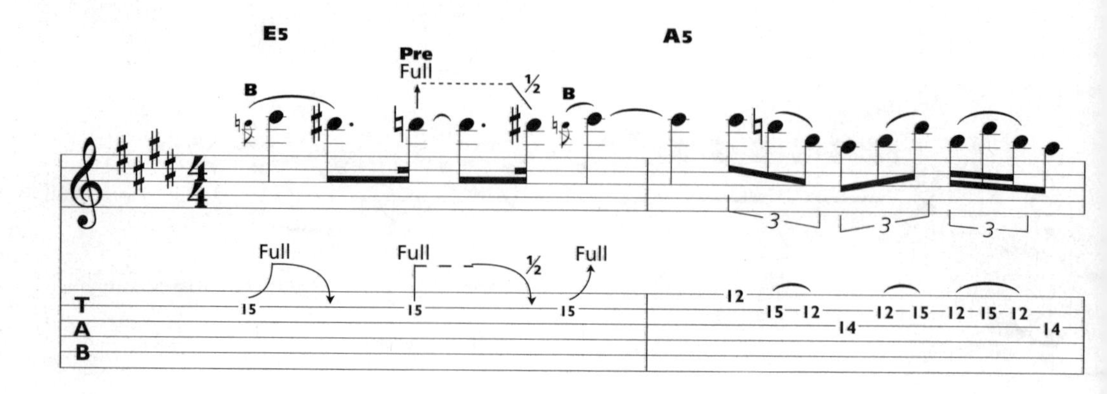

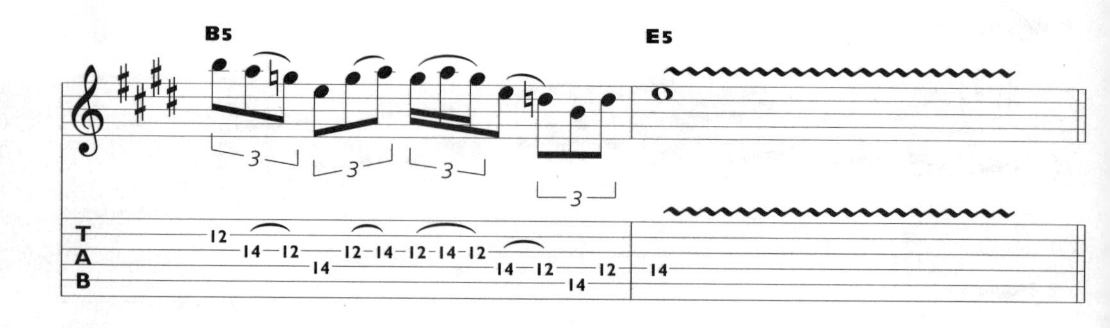

Select the bridge pickup, turn up the distortion and throw your head backwards for this **Gary Moore**-style pentatonic blast. Show how soulful you can be in the first bar, then cut to the chase with the embellished triplet lines in bar 2 and 3. When you feel confident enough, make them as fancy/widdly as you like.

Warning

You can only afford to show off like this once or twice per gig.

Gary Moore achieved technical mastery of many great playing techniques, including his trademark throw-your-head-back-and-screw-up-your-face string bending method.

The Trill Has Gone

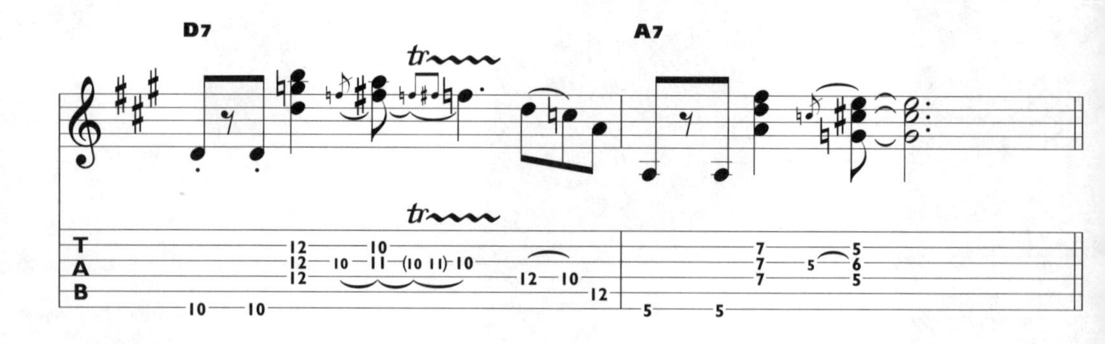

This is a multi-purpose lead/rhythm lick, with a distinctive bluesy major/minor feel. The trills should be relaxed and lazy, rather than fast and super-accurate. If you find yourself unsure of the direction an improvised solo is taking, reel it back in with this traditional-sounding but versatile idea.

To change key, simply move the whole shape around the fretboard.

Take Me Back Home

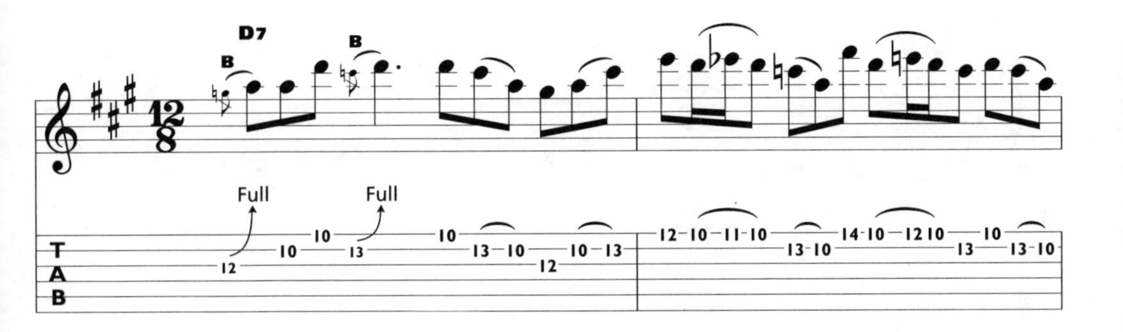

Most of the examples in this section will work over the '1' chord - i.e. if you're in the key of A, this will be a chord of A.

This one, however, is to be used over the '4' (i.e. the first time in a 12-bar that the chords change). To play this lick in a minor key, just move all the F♯'s down a fret to F natural and the final C♯ down to C.

Electric Showcase

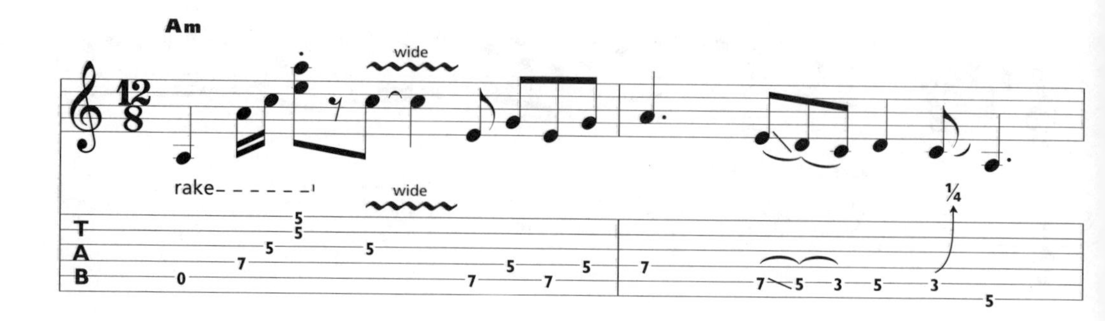

Take Note...

Notice how both open and fretted A notes are used side by side for a contrasting sound. Using the A blues scale, keep the pattern varied, even if you have to learn some 'improvised' variations beforehand.

This strongly rhythmic phrase features authentic embellishments like raked chords, wide vibrato and sliding position changes.

Sally Can't Wait

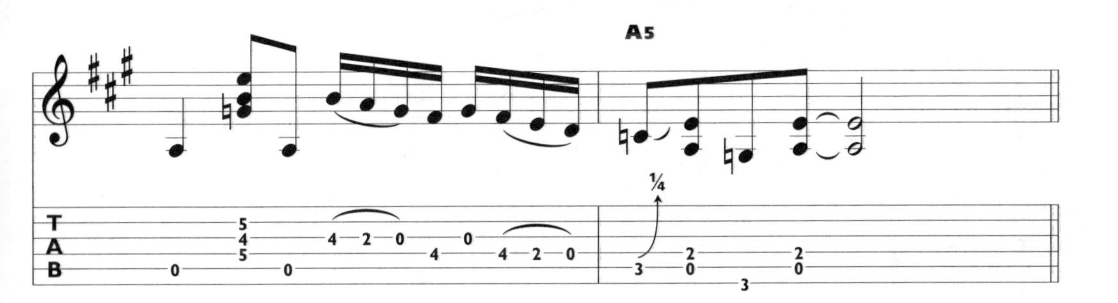

Here's a brisk **'Mustang Sally'** groove using a single sliding chord shape and pull-off embellishments. Overall the chord is A7, though some of the voicings step a little outside of this.

However, because they pass so quickly they don't register as different chords, so you can carry on soloing in true bluffer tradition using A minor pentatonic regardless.

Mississippi Time

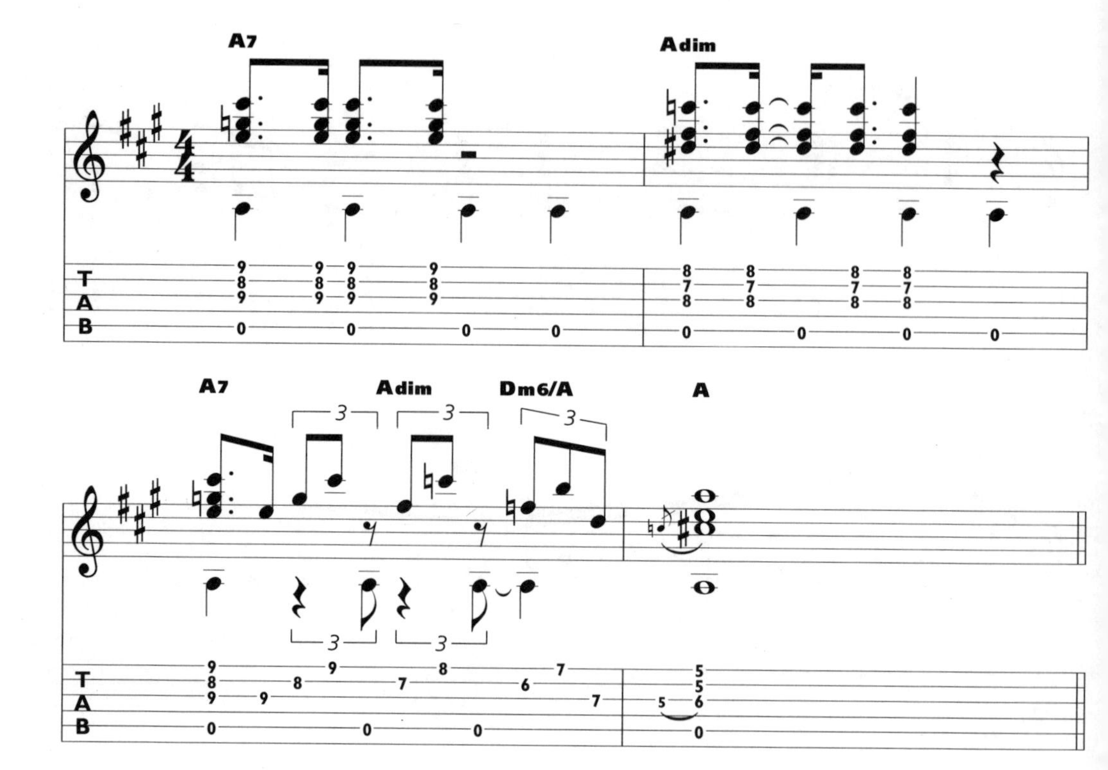

Here's an 'authentic' **Robert Johnson** intro/outro, using a descending D7 chord shape over the open fifth string - notated with the stems pointing downward down to signify that this part is played with your picking hand thumb.

There is a little rhythmic syncopation in the 3rd bar, so keep your foot tapping to avoid losing the thread. Hopefully the audience will think you've got a big Delta influence in your sound, and won't suspect for a second that you've got a problem with timekeeping.

Diminished Response

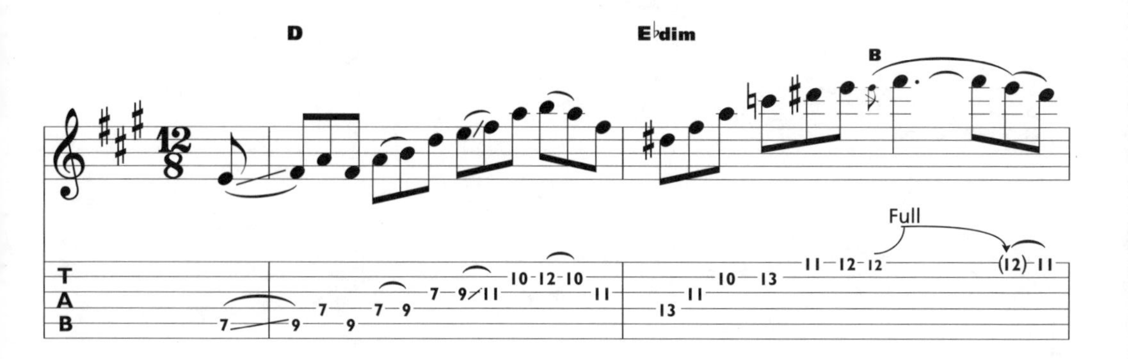

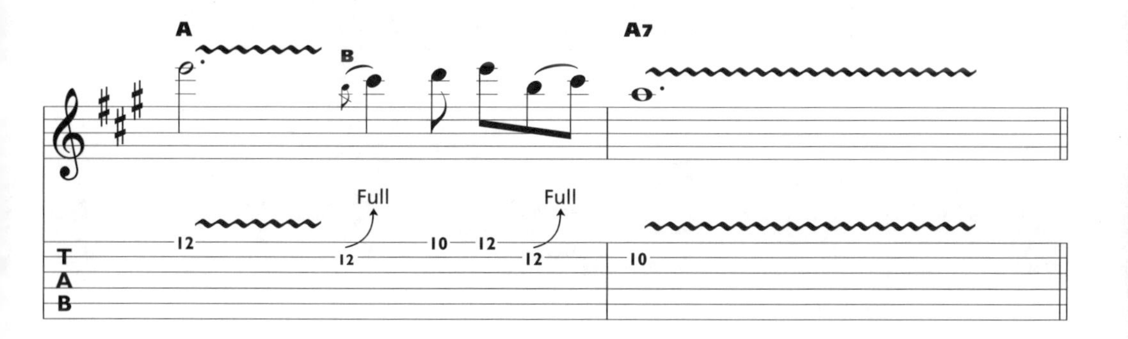

If you were wondering what to play over a diminished chord - as featured in a few of the examples - there are two ways to approach this. **Firstly**, you could ignore it - there is no need to play anything other than the blues or pentatonic scale. **Secondly**, you can try the diminished arpeggio shape featured at the beginning of bar two. Start with the root note (in this case E♭) and this will translate anywhere on the neck.

High-Speed Lenny

For the final example, here is a longer 9-bar phrase, showing the development of a theme, inserting solo fills in a similar way to **SRV**'s 'Scuttle Buttin'. This kind of approach is great for those times when you don't have a band with you, but want to show off anyway. For more on this, see page 81.

evie Ray Vaughan: Slick and polished - that's his playing, not his dress sense!

Chord Sequences or 'What, you mean there's more than one?'

There's a common misconception that the 12-bar is the only 'authentic' type of blues (you know the one I mean - play E for a while, move to A, then back to E. Finally, play B7, then A, then E, before playing the whole thing again. And again).

While there are many great tunes which use this format and its variations (**Blind Lemon**'s 'Matchbox Blues', **Robert Johnson**'s 'Crossroads Blues', **SRV**'s 'Pride & Joy' to name but three) it's also possible to play the blues using many chord changes (anything by **Steely Dan**) or none at all (**John Lee Hooker**).

Jamming Tip

When you're jamming along to a chord sequence at a gig, never, repeat NEVER, look at anyone in the band. If you make eye contact with another musician you'll lose that far-away look that keeps the audience believing that your playing is the result of a direct hotline to God.

Also, you mustn't be seen to look at another guitar player's hand to find out what chord they're playing (assume it's an E and you'll be right about 60% of the time, which is a better rate of accuracy than most jazz players, for example). If in doubt, keep your eyes closed. Just remember to open them every 32 bars or so to check that people aren't heading for the exits...

In this section you'll find several versions of the 'standard' 12-bar plus a few different sequences that crop up from time to time. All the chords are shown as fretboxes, and each example includes tips on how it can be used.

Standard 12-Bar In E

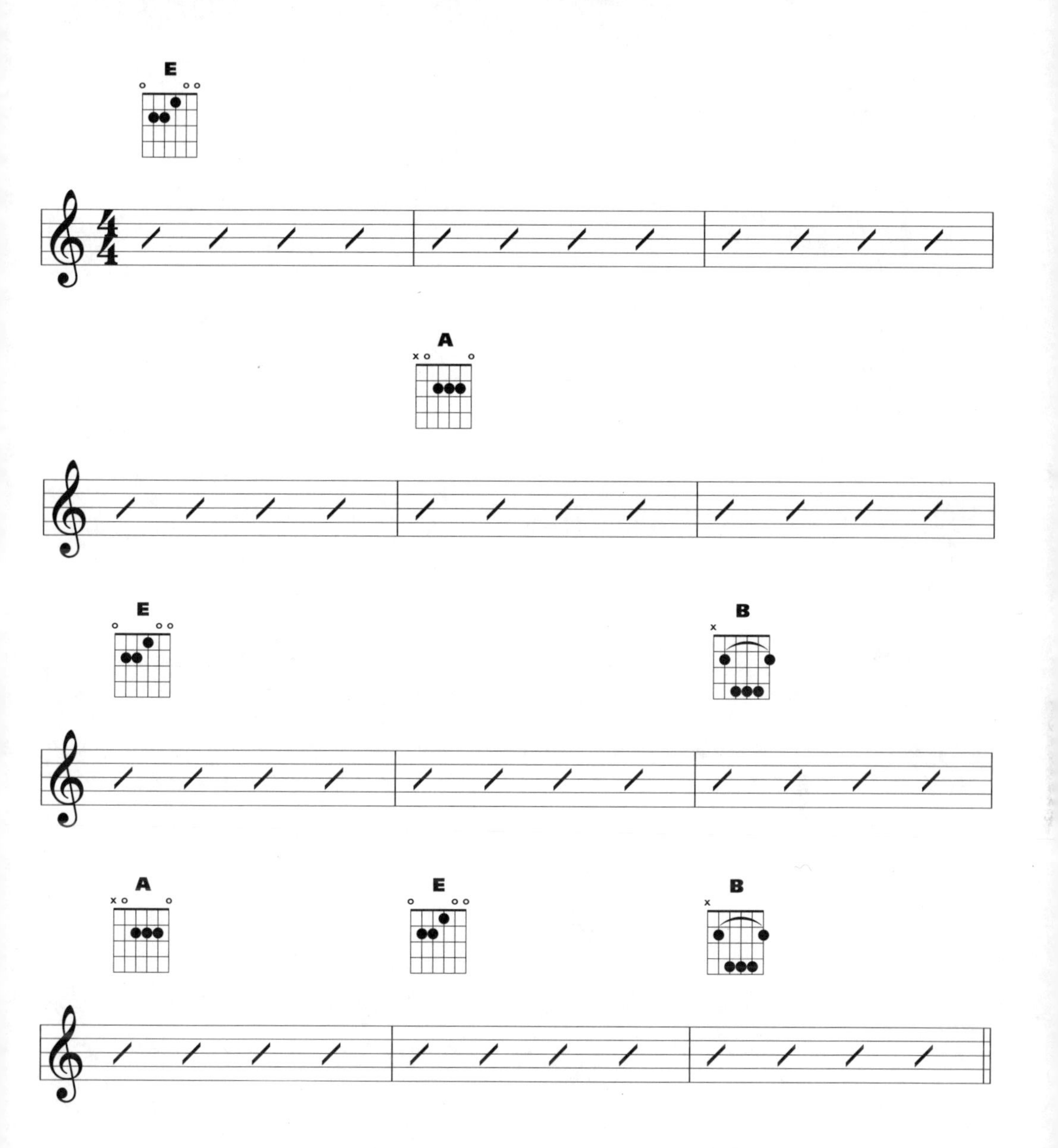

The best place to start has to be the standard **12 bar blues** pattern. Though this is shown as a four to the bar arrangement, it translates easily into any rhythmic feel. Try experimenting with a few of the rhythm patterns and/or dynamics and you will soon recognise the basic structure of many a blues standard.

Adding Changes

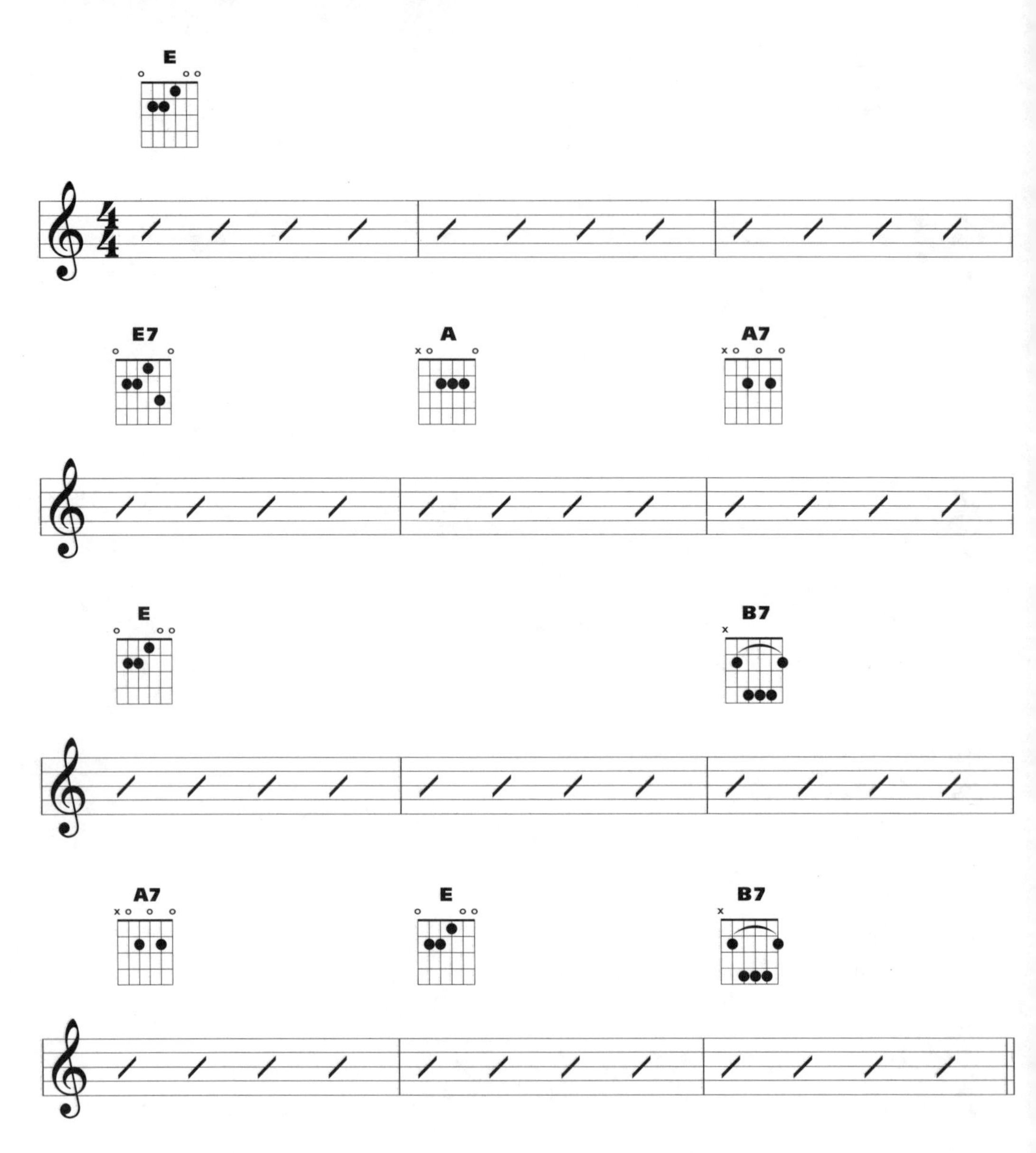

Take the standard 12 bar pattern and embellish it with a few extra chords to make the backing more interesting for the listener. Beware of taking this idea too far though - it's all too easy to cross the line into jazz, in which case you might have to put on a different style of hat mid-solo - **tricky**!

Peter Green 12-Bar

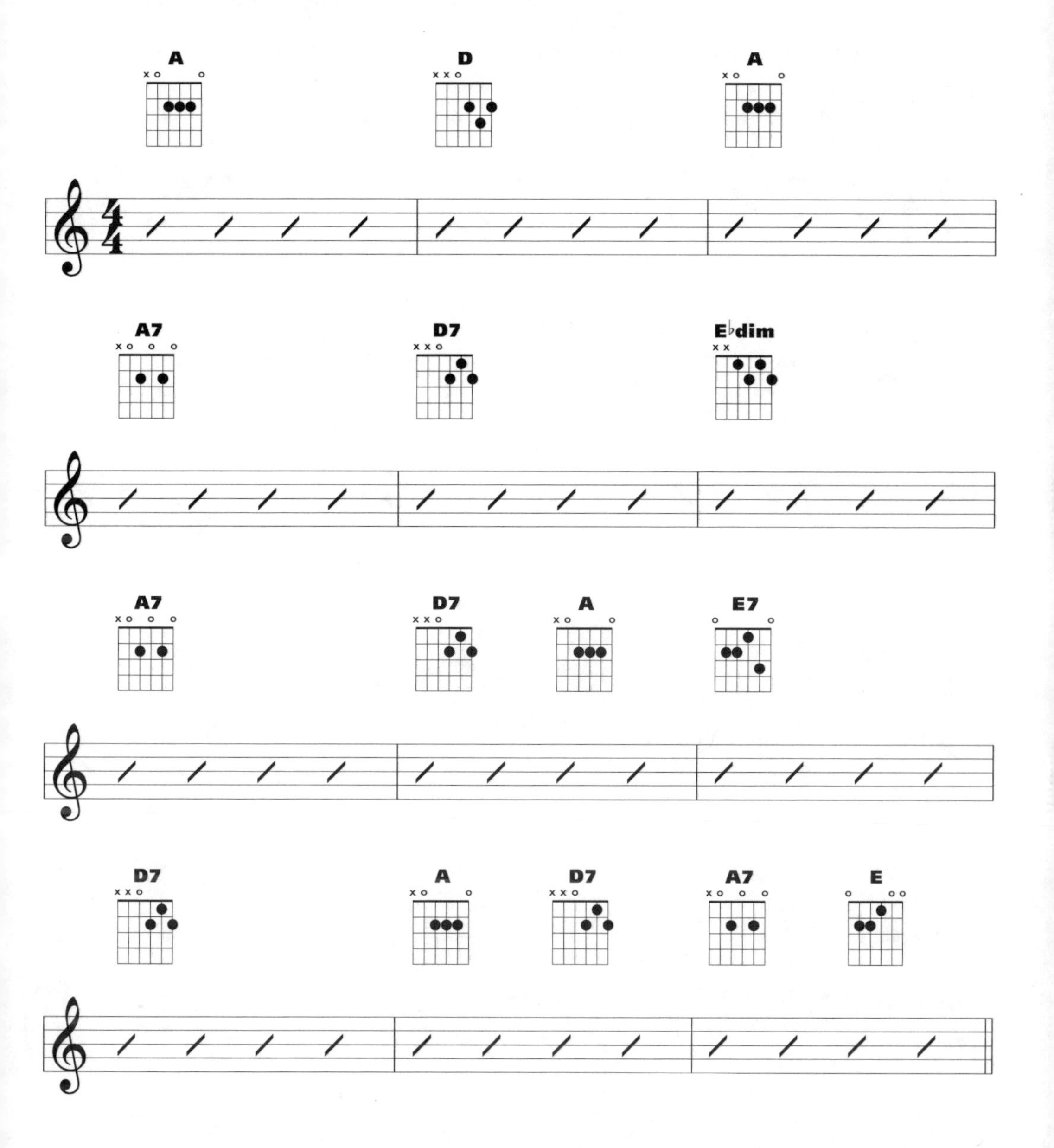

Here's another variation on the 12-bar, featuring a diminished chord voicing, as heard in **Peter Green/Fleetwood Mac**'s 'Need Your Love So Bad'. These chords can give a dramatic feel to an otherwise straight 'major' progression. The turnaround in the final two bars utilises the popular I IV I V figure (chords one, four, one and five, so if you're in A, that'll be A, D, A and E). Use Roman numerals to refer to chord numbers wherever possible - it confuses people and enhances your bluffing status.

Smart-Ass 12-Bar

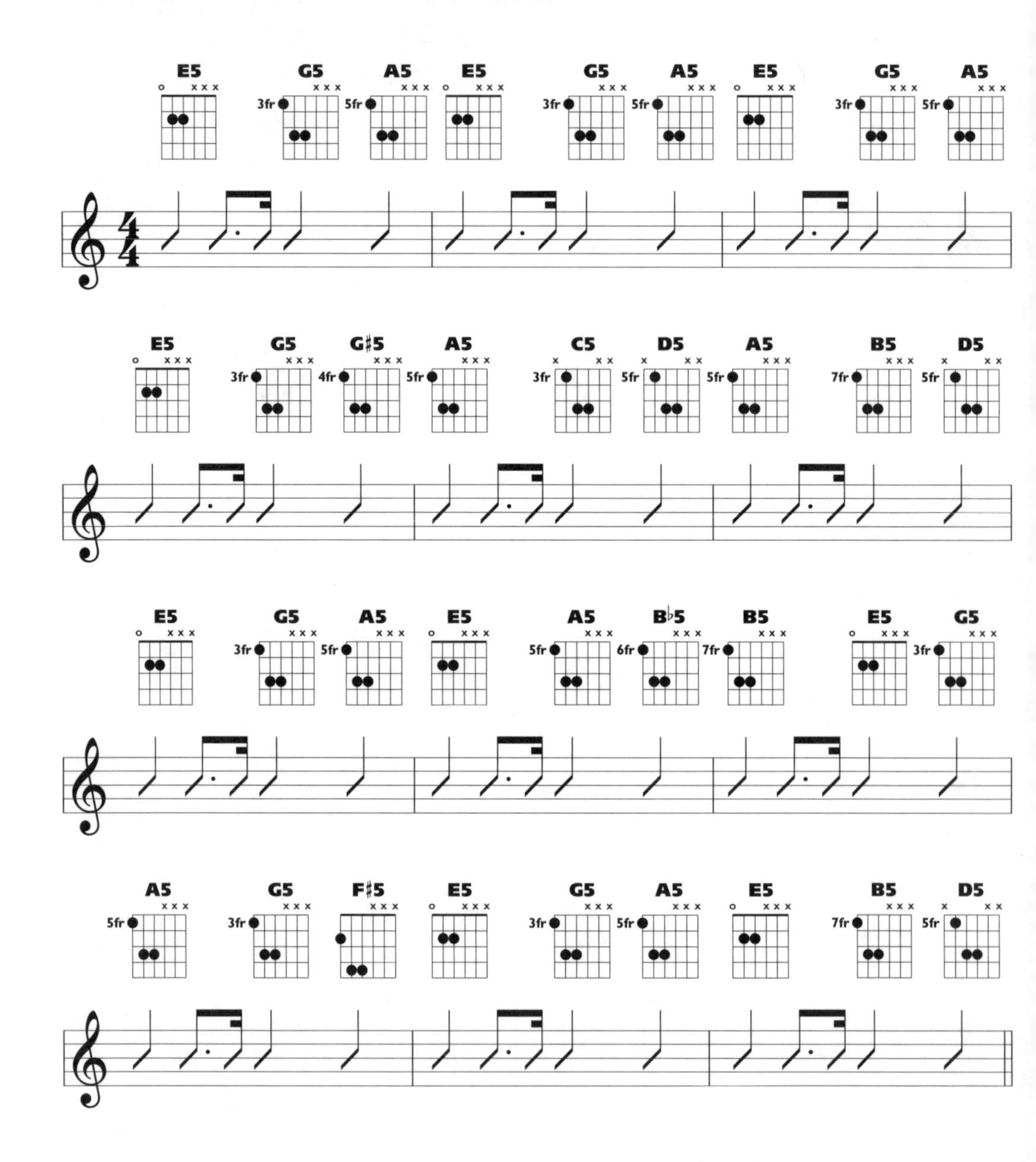

With a laid back shuffle rhythm, this sequence still follows the basic 12-bar pattern, but takes a riff-based approach to the chords. You'll find that it can be played in a variety of different ways, with many of the chords being interchangeable. It's great for impressing fellow band members with your extensive chord knowledge - **but try not to look smug!**

Slow Minor 12-Bar

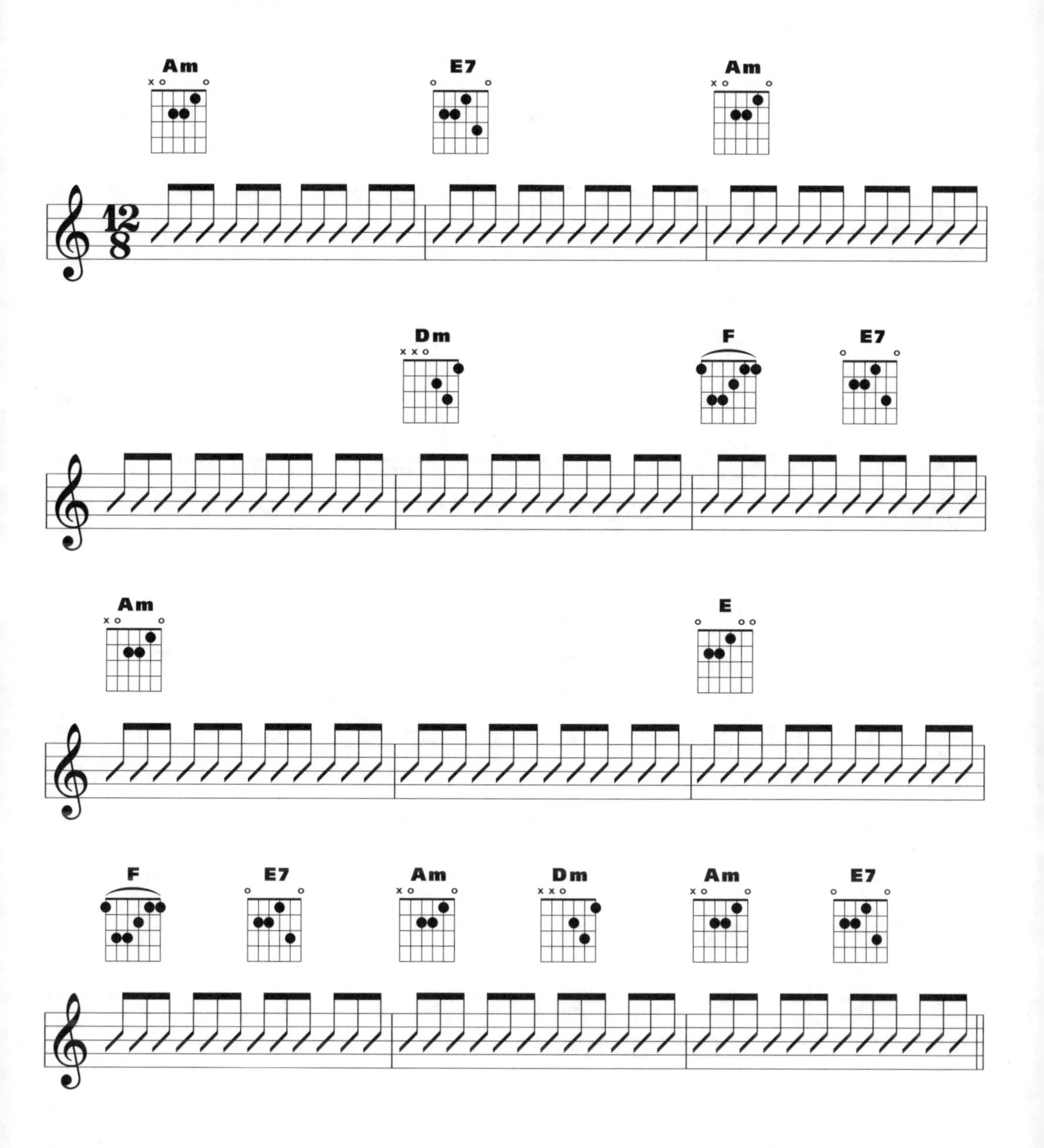

Though it's less common, a good minor blues progression is an **essential part of the blues bluffer's arsenal**. It also lends itself to wailing pentatonic solos like nothing else! This sequence works equally well at an incredibly slow pace, or taken up to a foot stomping shuffle. It uses a minor version of the same turnaround as the 'Peter Green 12-bar' on page 71.

BB's Ninth 12-Bar

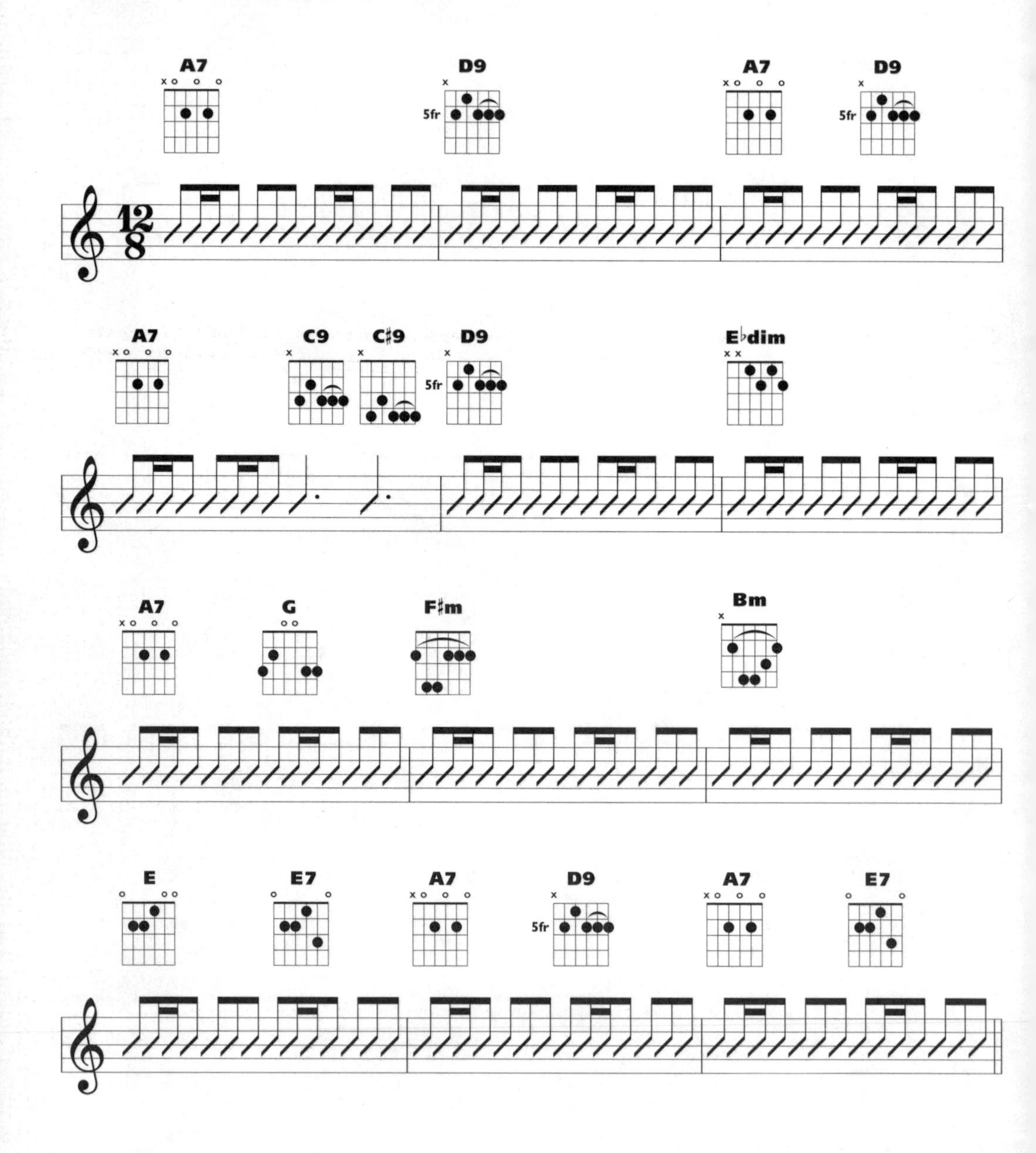

Though often associated with jazz, the 9th chord shown in this example has featured heavily in the music of **BB King** as far back as anyone can remember. It's fully interchangeable with a 7th chord, so can help you to avoid playing identical rhythm parts in every chorus. Being a small, easily moveable shape also makes it ideal for chromatic 'step' ideas, as shown in bar 4.

Bluesman **Jeff Healey** plays the guitar laid flat on his lap and knows all his scale shapes by touch alone.

Scales or 'What, you mean I have to use more than two fingers to play this lick?'

Yeah, yeah, I know. If you've got this far, you're probably good enough to bluff your way out of learning any theory, yes? I can hear cries of; "If you gonna play the blues, you gotta feel it, man, you don't need no book-larnin' music theory, my gran-pappy done' gone' tol' me if I feel the blues I just go with that feelin'..."

This is fine most of the time (and has worked for the likes of **John Lee**, **Blind Lemon**, **Willie Dixon** etc), but unfortunately, in the last 30-40 years electric blues players have simply become better. Don't blame the guitar teachers, blame the players. From **Peter Green**, **Hendrix** and **Eric Clapton** in the 1960s to **SRV**, **Robben Ford** and **Gary Moore** in the 1980s, the blues virtuoso is here to stay. And now and again you'll need to prove that you know what you're doing with scales.

In this section are eight scales which should give you a good overview of the different note choices that you can make in a solo, all shown in the key of E or A. Most guitar players already know the blues/minor pentatonic scale or one of its variants, but it's included here for those who are new to lead playing.

Good Idea!

Remember, once you can play the scale itself, you don't have to use the whole thing in your solo - sometimes as few as two or three notes can make a great lead lick over the chord backing.

These examples are by no means exhaustive - the blues scale of E, for example, can be played in at least 7 different positions (including sitting on your front porch with a bottle of beer) - but they will make you look good. Any blues guitarist who sees you play all eight of these shapes in one gig will think you a true blues master.

All scale fretboxes are shown upright, with the headstock at the top, and the strings ascending in pitch from left to right: i.e. **the lowest E string is on the left.**

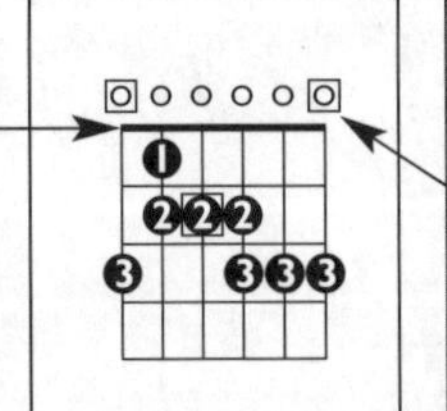

A box around a note or open string simply means that note is a 'root' note. E.g. **in A major any boxed out notes will be A.**

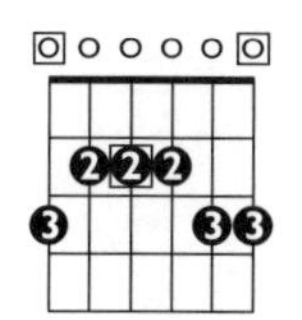

Em Pentatonic Scale

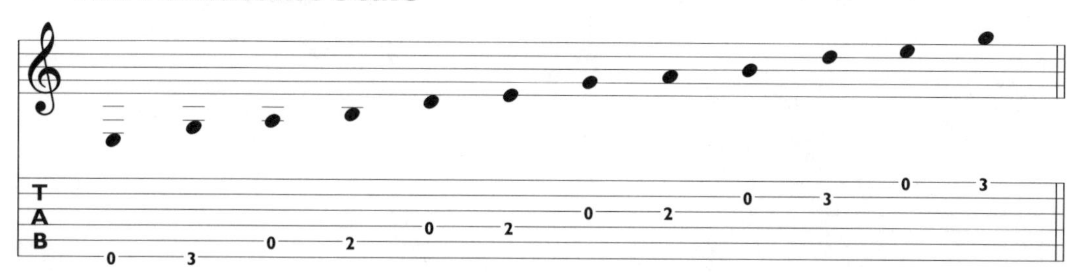

Without question the most essential scale shape bar none! The minor pentatonic scale is the basis of countless solos, riffs and even songs. Prominent users include players as diverse as John Lee Hooker, Jimmy Page and Albert King. This is the open E version - the most popular shape, in the most popular key.

E Blues Scale

Staying with the same idea, this is the Blues scale, also in the key of E. As you can see, it's basically the same as the minor pentatonic with an added note in two places. This is known as the flat fifth (♭5). This one note gives that classic mean 'n' moody blues vibe - even if you simply play up and down the scale.

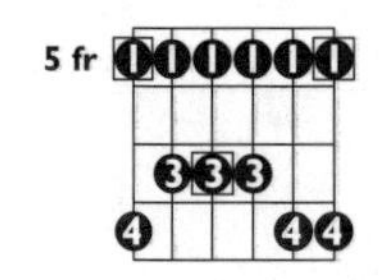

Am Pentatonic Scale

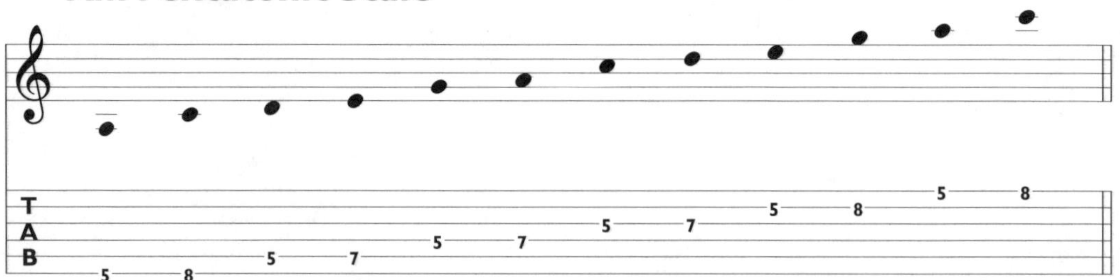

To demonstrate how easy the minor pentatonic scale is to use, take a look at this version in the key of A. If you use your first finger for all the notes on the fifth fret, the pattern is easily recognisable as a fretted version of the E minor pentatonic. Simply add a whole tone bend at the 7th fret of the third string when running through this, and you're playing a solo!

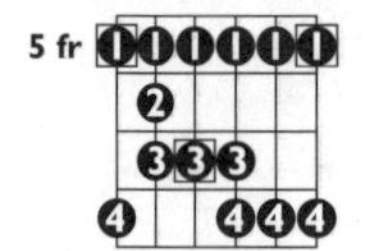

A Blues Scale

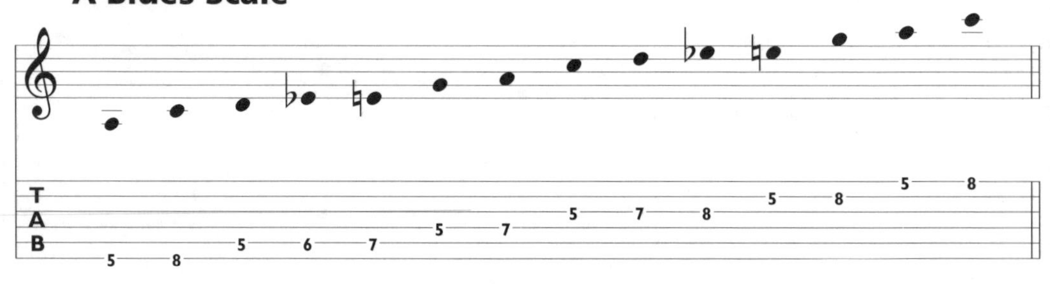

Here is the Blues scale again, this time in the key of A. The ♭5 note in this key is E♭. Try bending the third string as described in the previous example, then try bending it just a semitone (one fret's worth) for real blues authenticity.

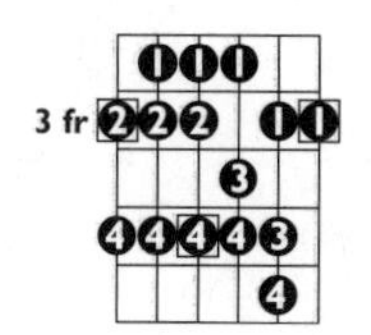

G Mixolydian Mode

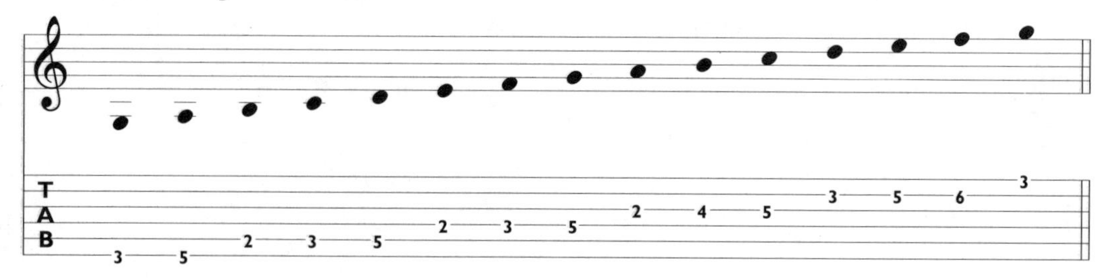

This scale is known as the G Mixolydian mode, or if that sounds a bit scary, G major with the 7th note flattened. This means the seventh note of the scale - normally F♯ - is lowered to F natural, making this version of the scale much more usable than the standard major pattern in a blues context. Try nailing that F note over a G7 chord, to draw admiring glances from other guitarists.

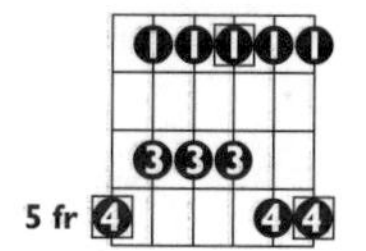

A Major Pentatonic

Playing blues licks in a major key can be a hazardous business. A minor pentatonic would almost fit over an A major based blues, but there would be some questionable moments; e.g., a C natural coinciding with the C♯ contained in an A major chord! To avoid these problems, try this A major pentatonic scale. All your favourite bending licks etc will fit beautifully, without you having to avoid any notes in the pattern.

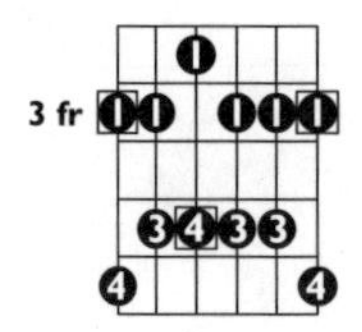

Am Pentatonic with Major 6th

This variation of the A minor pentatonic is used and much loved by **BB King** and **Robben Ford**. It features an F♯ where there would usually be a G, and can be used to give a dramatic 'outside' almost jazzy effect. It works especially well if you are playing over bass and drums only, as there's no instrument defining the major/minor chord backing, meaning that any old bluffing around using this shape will sound credible.

Em Pentatonic Scale

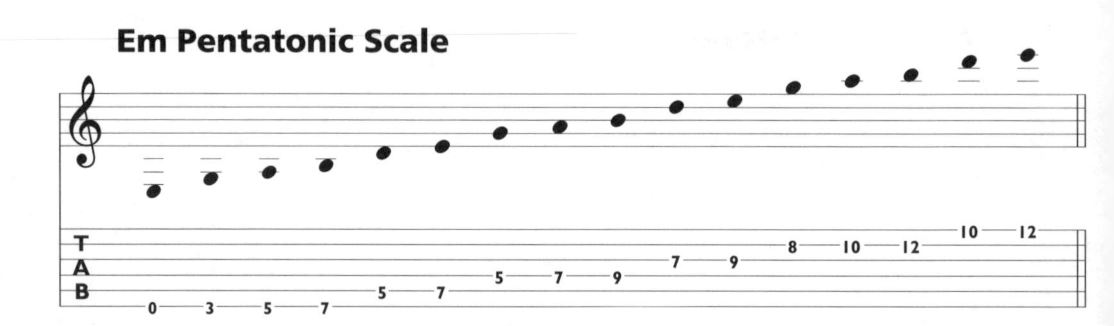

If you only ever learn one scale shape, make it this one! Spanning three whole octaves, from the open sixth string to the twelfth fret of the first, it incorporates elements of all the minor pentatonic scale positions along the fretboard. Though it works best as featured, in the key of E, parts of it can be transposed into any key.

Music Shop Classic or 'How do I fit everything in this book into 24 bars of showing off?'

Here is a specially designed party piece, guaranteed to impress next time you're in a guitar shop. Arranged in answering phrases like many a classic blues track, the feel is reminiscent of John Lee Hooker's 'Boom Boom'.

It begins with some open position pull-offs, and this main riff is kept strongly in evidence for the first 12 bars, which also contains elements of **Hubert Sumlin**, **Robert Johnson** and **Freddie King**. Around the halfway mark, a few more modern influences creep in, like **Eric Clapton**, **Gary Moore**, **SRV** and **Kenny Wayne Shepherd**. Here, the riff takes more of a back seat, as it has been strongly established by now, and besides, by this point you'll have drawn a crowd anyway...

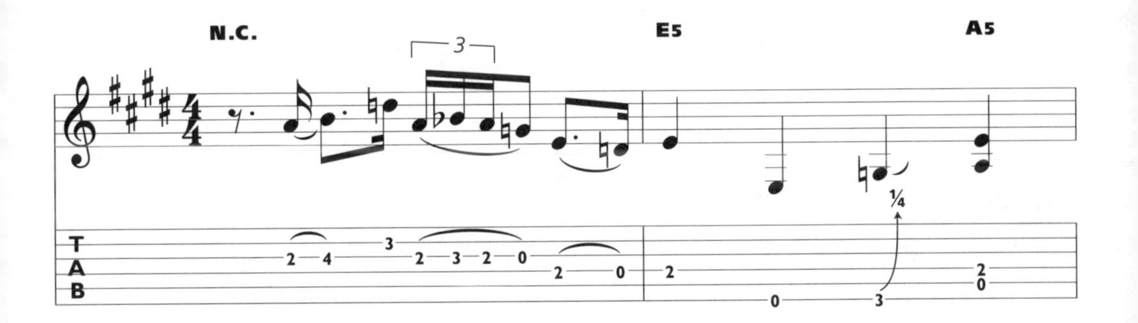

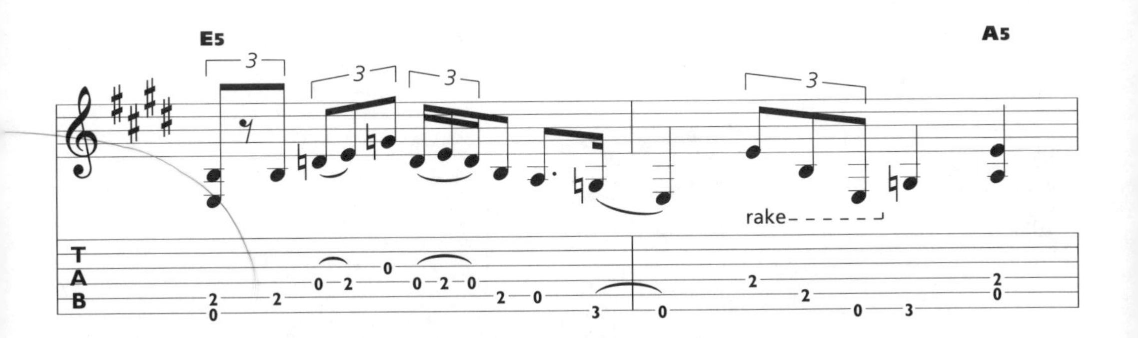

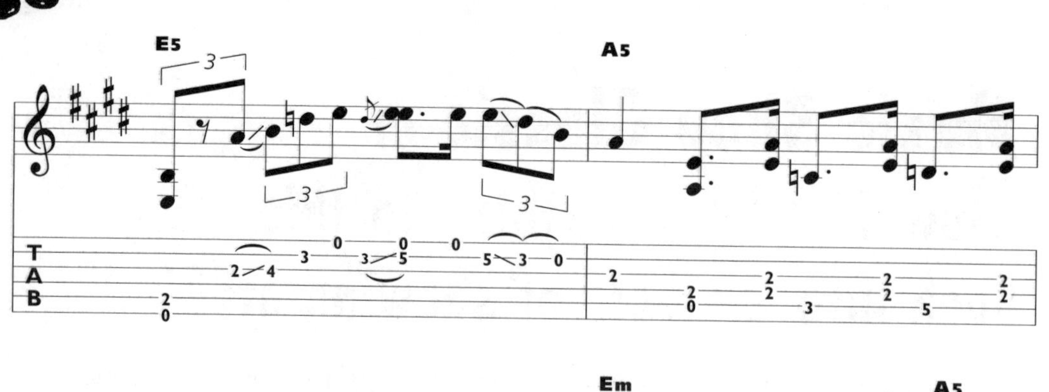
E5
A5

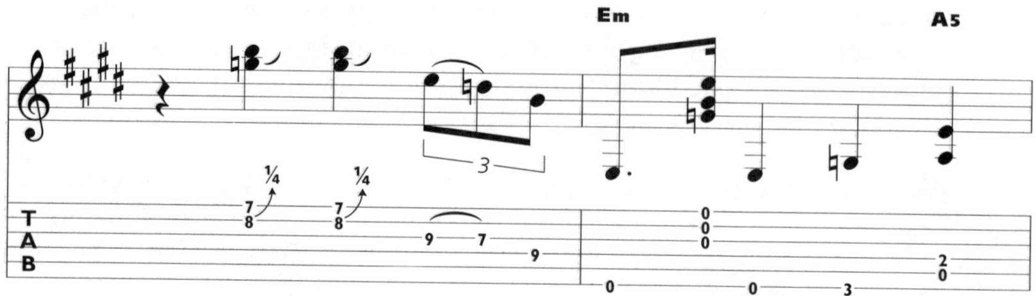
Em
A5
¼
¼

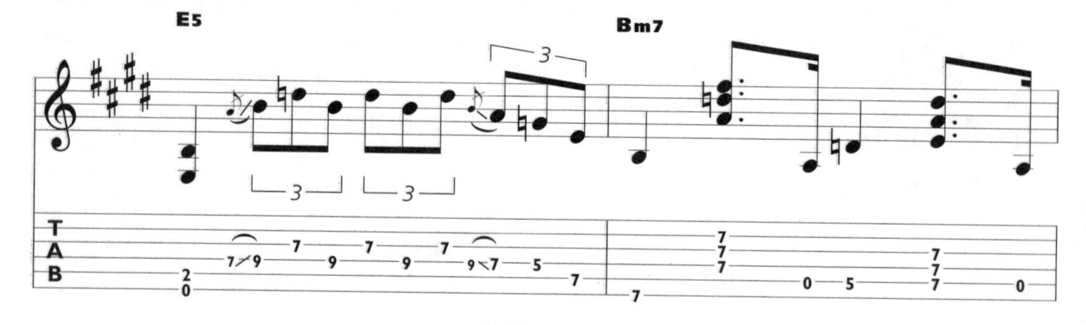
E5
Bm7

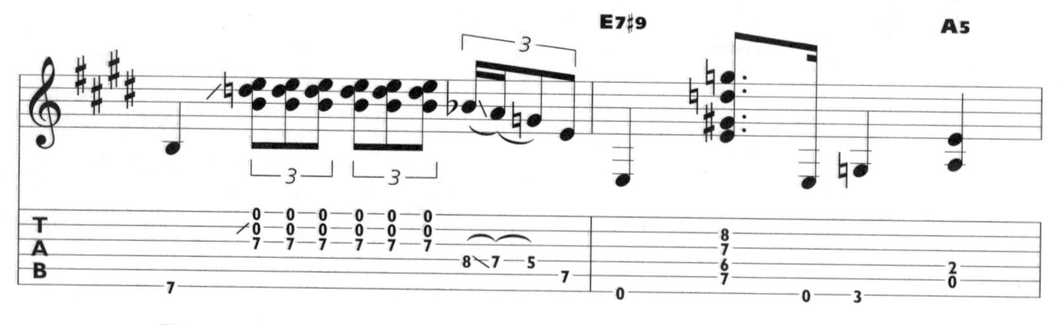
E7♯9
A5

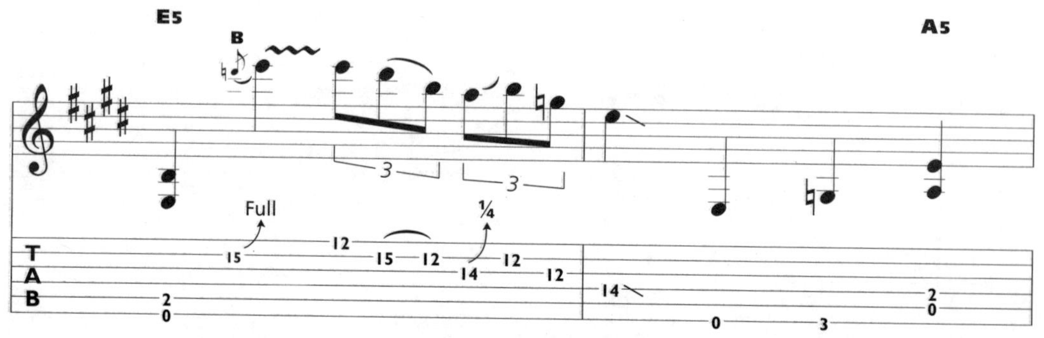
E5
B
A5
Full
¼

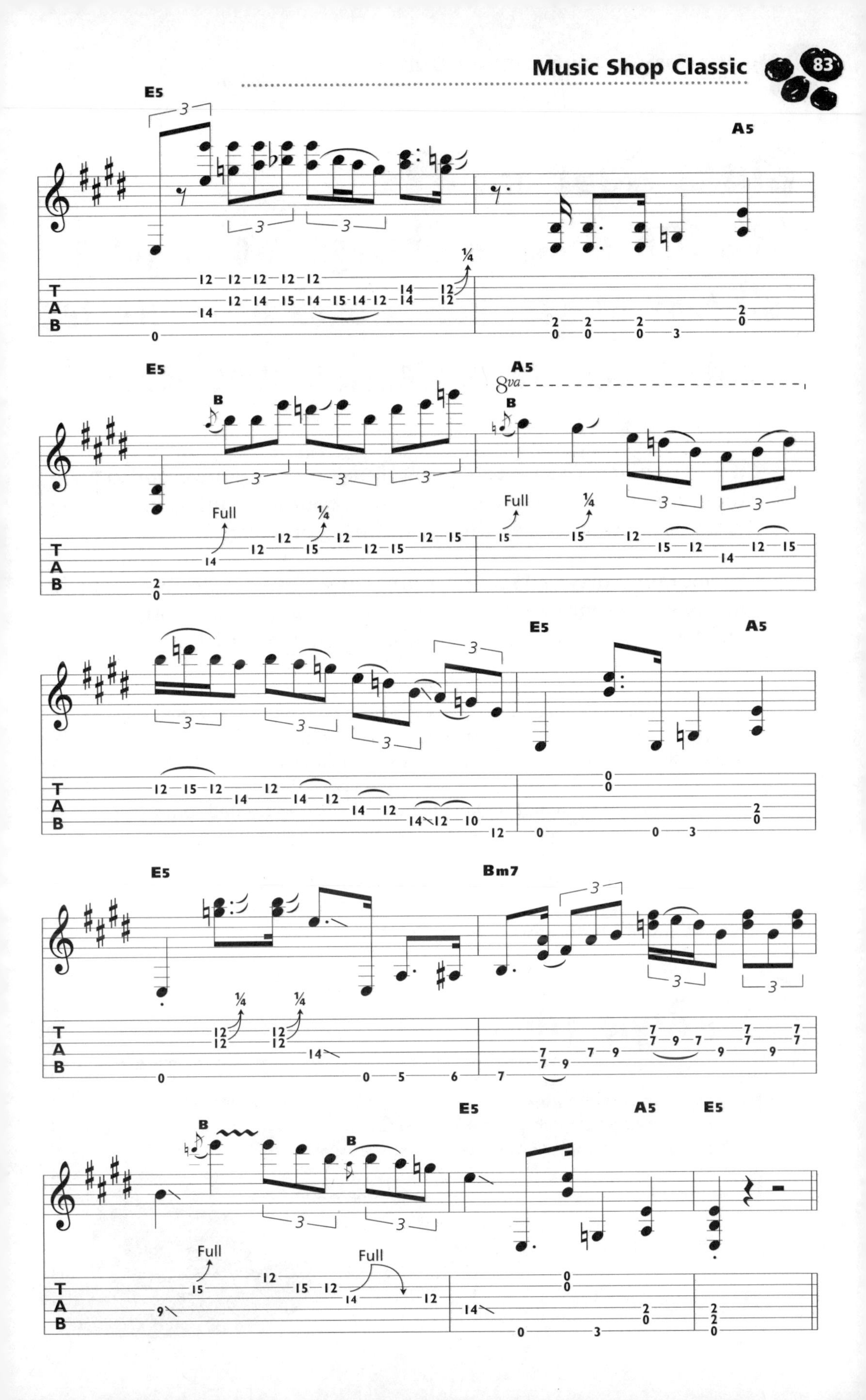
E5
A5
E5
A5
8va
B
Full
¼
E5
A5
E5
Bm7
E5
A5
E5
B
Full
T
A
B

Blues Gear or "It's 106 miles to Chicago, we've got a full tank of gas, half a pack of cigarettes, it's dark and we're wearing sunglasses."

'The Blues Brothers' motion picture

If you're going to be a convincing blues player, you've got to have the right gear, which means thinking about everything from string gauge to guitar style to the type of hat you wear.

Iconography plays a big part in this - it's perfectly OK, for example, to say you bought a Gibson semi-solid because Freddie King plays one (even if you really got it because you like Oasis!).

In this section you'll find a list of all the gear you ought to buy, plus some tips on how to set up your equipment to recreate typical blues tones. Naturally, not everyone can afford a roomful of vintage amps, so there are also some tips on how to program a humble home multi-fx unit with a variety of blues guitar sounds.

If you do own a rack full of flashing lights and electronic sound-sculpturing equipment, stick the whole thing in an orange box or beer crate. If your amp is emblazoned with the words 'Authentic Tube Sound Blues King Valve Tone Classic', then it was almost certainly made by androids in a Korean micro-chip factory sometime last year, so you'll need to disguise it a little (take off the logo, wrap the whole thing in canvas, leave it out in the rain for a year or so etc).

Style Tip

As with most blues bluffing, how it all sounds is unimportant. Make sure that you and your gear look good on stage, and the audience will convince themselves that they've just seen a master at work.

Jake and **Elwood Blues** - the only gear they needed was a Cadillac, two pairs of sunglasses and a Mission from God.

What to Wear

HAT Any sort of headwear is instant cool in blues-land - this classic hat-trick has been used by John Lee, Jimi and Stevie Ray, among many others.

SHADES (black) Opinion is divided as to whether a blues dude should wear shades. They look cool, sure, but can put your bluffing at a disadvantage - the audience won't be able to see you wince convincingly when you're 'playing with feel'.

GUITAR Safe bets are the Gibson 335 (if you're black) or Fender Strat (if you're white). No-one's quite sure where this racial segregation began, but only a very small number of players have opposed it; Robert Cray and Jimi Hendrix (black guys with Strats), and occasionally Clapton (began with a Gibson 335, but even he gave in to tradition and went back to Strats in the 1970s).

JACKET Most classic blues players are pretty well-dressed - from Blind Lemon right through to Clapton, well-tailored jackets have always been the order of the day. Get one that's a couple of sizes too big - you'll look like you haven't eaten in a week.

TROUSERS Cotton suit trousers only. Denim takes you more in an R&B direction... anything leather, and you're an instant rock poseur.

SHOES Keep them clean. If you're feeling confident, you can make up a story about your days as a Chicago shoeshine boy in the 1950s (not recommended for young bluffers unless your audience has a serious problem with maths).

Guitars and Amps or Trainspotter's corner

With the current level of technology available to the guitarist, you could argue that it's possible to make any guitar produce just about any sound desired.

However, if this view were widely held by most players, the guitar manufacturing industry (not to mention the blues bluffing industry) would collapse. Endless hours of fun can be had debating whether the type of dot-marker on the neck of an **ES-335** improves its tone, or whether a '54 Strat would really beat a '57 in a straight fight. However, if you're going to prove your blues pedigree, a working knowledge of the guitars themselves is a must. There are three major contenders for the 'blues axe' crown – the **Gibson ES-335**, the **Fender Stratocaster**, and the **Gibson Les Paul**.

Eyes shut and frown!

Background information on each has been provided, including famous users, instant opinion, and a knowledgeable fact which you can use as evidence of your blues guitar aptitude. **All usage of jargon has, of course, been maximised for your convenience.**

Gibson ES-335

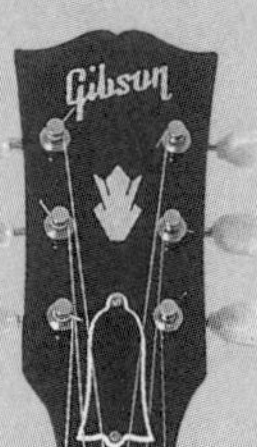

ANORAK DATA:
First introduced in 1958 as the ES-335T. Spawned the rest of the (similar) '300' series - the ES-355, 345 and 325 (so be very careful about talking about a '335' unless you're sure that's what it is - this is a guaranteed way for your bluffer's mask to be exposed). Also note: The Gibson-owned Epiphone company do NOT make a 335. If you see a 335 lookalike with the Epiphone logo, it's most likely to be a Riviera or a Sheraton.

FAMOUS NAMES:
BB King, Freddie King, Eric Clapton (with Cream), John Lee Hooker (with a bottle of beer), Alvin Lee.

DESIGN:
Solid centre block. Two humbucking pickups with three-way selector switch. Two volume plus two tone controls.

SOUND:
Despite the semi-solid construction, fundamentally a 335 sounds and feels like an electric guitar. Adjectives to use include 'warm', 'mellow' etc, plus more esoteric words like 'soulful', 'emotional', 'mild'. Or you can use the catch-all term 'evocative' - no-one will dare challenge its use in fear that they won't know exactly what a 335 evokes (in a crisis, this word can be used to refer to any guitar).

KNOWLEDGEABLE FACT:
Often called a 'semi-acoustic' but this is sometimes confused with 'electro-acoustic'. The correct definition is 'semi-solid', due to the solid centre block which runs along the length of the guitar to reduce feedback.

INSTANT OPINION:
"The trapeze tailpiece model definitely has more sustain." (untrue, but impossible to prove without an oscilloscope).

ACCEPTABLE CRITICISM:
A brand new ES335TD is phenomenally expensive (around £1600 in the UK or $3,300 in the USA).

Opinion is divided over whether those dot-shaped neck markers affect the tone...

Gibson Les Paul

ANORAK DATA:
First introduced in 1952 ('Gold Top' model). Designed by the eponymous guitarist. Humbuckers replaced single-coil pickups in 1957. Various off-shoots (Les Paul Junior, Les Paul Special, Les Paul Deluxe etc) but the two best-known are the Standard and Custom.

FAMOUS NAMES:
Eric Clapton (Bluesbreakers), Gary Moore, Jimmy Page, Paul Kossoff.

DESIGN:
Solid body (originally mahogany) with arched top, two humbucking pickups with three-way selector switch. Two volume, two tone controls.

SOUND:
Les Paul wanted the guitar to have a 20-second sustain (hence the mahogany), and this is the instrument's most famous characteristic. Combination of solid construction and high-output pickups makes it suitable for high-gain, long distorted sounds (hence the rock-blues leanings of the above-named players). Typical adjectives include 'singing', 'ringing', 'stinging', 'swinging' (jazzers only), 'gunslinging' (guitar heroes only).

KNOWLEDGEABLE FACT:
Some 'Les Pauls' have double cutaways and a flat top - these are referred to as 'SG-style'. Generally, though, the name Les Paul is used by players to describe the arch-top, single-cutaway guitar shown in the photo.

INSTANT OPINION:
Just say any old rubbish involving sustain, e.g. "the sustain on my old LP, it's incredible, but that's 'cos I got mine from a bloke who knew the milkman who used to deliver to Clapton's house back in '64."

ACCEPTABLE CRITICISM:
Try wearing a solid mahogany guitar on a shoulder strap throughout a 2-hour gig, then come up with your own...

The Les Paul Gold Top - ringing, singing, and gunslinging.

Fender Stratocaster

ANORAK DATA:
First introduced in 1954. Design has hardly changed in 45 years. Some models manufactured in Japan from early 1980s, under the Squier brand name. Strats are now made in the following countries (listed in order of price and quality): USA, Japan, Korea, Mexico, and China.

FAMOUS NAMES:
Jeff Beck, Eric Clapton (solo albums), Ry Cooder, Robert Cray, Rory Gallagher, Peter Green, Jimi Hendrix, Kenny-Wayne Shepherd, Stevie Ray Vaughan.

DESIGN:
3 single-coil pickups, double-cutaway, solid body. Floating bridge vibrato unit (though this is not used by many blues players).

SOUND:
Generally brighter than other blues guitars, due to its single-coil pickups. Adjectives to use include 'sparkling', 'glassy', 'sharp', 'honking', 'bell-like', 'squealing', 'crisp'...

KNOWLEDGEABLE FACT:
Single-ply scratchplates were replaced by three-play white/black/white versions in 1959. Impress other Strat users by noting that their single-ply scratchplate (very common on copies) is "based on the classic '57 design".

INSTANT OPINION:
"Early '80s Japanese Squiers were actually better made than the American Strats at the time." (true in some cases, and vague enough to convince everyone with your confident use of such a sweeping statement).

ACCEPTABLE CRITICISM:
They don't always stay in tune if you get carried away with the whammy bar.

This is a 1956 'Sunburst', but then you knew that by looking at the scratchplate, didn't yo

Backup Bluffs

And just in case...

If someone asks you about any other guitar, it's usually safest to steer the conversation back to one of the 'big three' by saying something like: "Yeah, I know what you mean about the Delectrolux Tri-Tonic Sound-u-Like model, but it can't really replace the warm tone of a real 335..."

However, if you get really stuck, here are a few bite-size snippets on other blues guitars:

1. Hollow-bodies

(Gibson, Epiphone, Gretsch, Guild)

F-hole hollow-bodies began in the 1940s. Deeper body than 335-types, known as 'thinlines', but genuinely hollow. Wood-like tone.

Prone to feedback, so better for 'clean' blues sounds. As used by **Howlin' Wolf**, **T-Bone Walker** and sometimes **John Lee Hooker**.

T-Bone Walker - hollow-bodied guitar showmanship.

2. Gibson Flying V

Solid-body, launched in 1958.
Not generally thought of as a blues guitar, but included here because it was played by left-handed bluesman **Albert King**.

Pickups and bridge identical to a Les Paul, but with V-shaped body.

The legendary **Albert King** - the most famous blues player ever to sport a **Flying V**.

3. Gibson Firebird

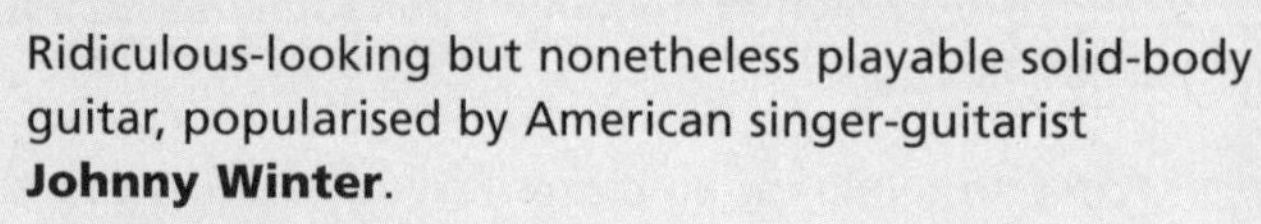

Ridiculous-looking but nonetheless playable solid-body guitar, popularised by American singer-guitarist **Johnny Winter**.

Vintage models sometimes feature bridge vibratos. Available in 'standard' and 'reverse' models (presumably the original shape was so awful that someone suggested swapping it round. It didn't improve things.)

Ridiculous-looking but well-loved
(that's the **Gibson Firebird**, not **Johnny Winter**).

Multi-FX settings

Shown here are suggested settings for a multi-FX unit. As all of these products have different specifications and names for settings, each parameter setting is shown as a percentage which should be translated into numbers according to whatever scale your multi-FX unit uses.

The only effects shown are distortion/overdrive, EQ and reverb. Don't use any others - remember, you're using all of this technology to create the sound of an amp in a room! Although we've suggested a guitar type, don't worry if the one you own is different - just follow the pickup settings shown anyway.

Guitar	distortion type	drive (%)	level (%)	low (%)	mid (%)	high (%)	rev type	rev length	rev level	sound
Semi-solid (e.g. 335) any pickup	overdrive	40	50	40	50	65	Hall	1.8s	20%	**BB King** smooth lead
Semi-solid (e.g. 335) neck pickup	overdrive	10	60	50	50	40	Room	1.0s	10%	**John Lee Hooker** Rhythm
Strat neck pickup	overdrive	30	70	40	70	60	Hall	2.0s	40%	**Peter Green** slow blues
Strat neck pickup	overdrive	10	80	50	40	60	Room	1.2s	15%	**Robert Cray** '80s
Strat neck pickup	overdrive/ sustain/lead	65	50	40	70	35	Hall	1.8s	30%	**Clapton** '70s
Strat mid pickup	blues or overdrive	50	50	60	60	40	Room	1.0s	20%	**SRV** lead sound
Les Paul bridge pickup	overdrive	60	40	50	60	50	Hall	1.5s	20%	**Clapton** '60s 335 distortion
Les Paul neck pickup	overdrive/ sustain/lead	80	50	60	60	50	Hall	1.5s	30%	**Gary Moore** '80s

Blues Lyrics or 'My baby's still with me, I got a house and a car, and the sun's shining - guess I better join a pop band'

Most guitarists have a problem with lyrics, mainly because the words have a habit of filling that 24-bar section between the end of the intro and the start of the solo, taking up space which could easily feature more guitar parts.

However, it's a rare blues artist that makes his or her name purely from instrumentals, and sooner or later you're going to have to sing - or worse still, write - blues lyrics of your own.

Handy Hint

The first thing to remember is that (unlike any other type of songwriting) you don't have to avoid clichés. The classic blues idea of 'my baby left me' has been used by pretty much every guitarist mentioned in this book. Similarly, no rhyme is too obvious. **Stevie Ray** told his woman **"You can't change it, can't re-arrange it"**. **Peter Green** needed **"someone's hands to lead me through the night"** and **"someone's arms to hold me tight"**. **John Lee Hooker** even got away with rhyming the words **'Boom Boom'** with the words **'Boom Boom'**.

Repetition is actually desirable most of the time. Repetition is actually desirable most of the time. Not only can you almost always repeat verse 1 at the end of any blues to save you from writing another verse, you can actually repeat lines within the verse itself. The classic three-line blues is actually a two-line blues - the first two lines are the same.

Lyrical genius...

Check out **Blind Lemon Jefferson's** 'Matchbox Blues';
"I'm sittin' here wonderin', matchbox hole in my coat,
I'm sittin' here wonderin', matchbox hole in my coat,
I ain't got no matches but I sure got a long way to go"

Not exactly Shakespeare, and whoever said that 'coat' rhymes with 'go' anyway? However, one listen to Lemon's original (or even **Ringo Starr**'s painful version of **Carl Perkins**' version) and you'll be convinced that this man really *feels* that he, er, hasn't got any matches.

Contrary to popular belief, you can't just think about something that's upset you and assume it's good material for blues. Some subjects will lead you more towards Rock 'n' Roll (e.g. you can't have a blues lyric about automobiles, sex, high school etc). Others have already been snapped up by Country players (so avoid writing about orphans, dogs, disability, or deaf and blind dogs with no parents etc).

Sometimes even the way you describe the subject affects the style of music. 'Drink a wee glass of malt?' Scottish folk song. 'Take another cup of moonshine?' Country song. 'Need a shot of booze?' Heavy metal. And, of course, if you hadn't guessed already, the blues version should be 'got a bottle of bourbon'.

Generally, if you want to write blues lyrics, remember three things. Choose a subject that's a bit of a downer, but not life-threatening (say, running out of matches). Talk about it as if you were born in America, not Milton Keynes (don't 'pop to the supermarket'; instead, you should 'hang out in the local store'). And most importantly, sing it like you mean it. The more sincerity in your voice, the less anyone will pay attention to what you're actually singing.

2/05 (54004)

Outro

So now you've got it all - the background information, the CD collection, the licks, the techniques, the gear, and the lyrics. All you need now is a gig, and a blues gig is about as difficult to find as a policeman when you're illegally parked. Almost any bar which has live music will take on an untried blues band.

All you need to do is walk in and ask. As long as you're wearing the right clothes and you bluff your way with enough confidence, they probably won't even ask to hear a demo tape. Unless, of course, they've also got a copy of this book.

JOE BENNETT has been teaching guitar for fifteen years, and regularly works as a session guitarist. He is also a senior examiner in electric guitar for The London College of Music and Head of Popular Music at City of Bath College. Joe's publications include the *Guitar: To Go!* and *Really Easy Guitar* series, and *The Little Book of Scales*, plus tracks and articles for *Future Music*, *PowerOn* and *Total Guitar* magazines.

www.musicsales.com